surprised by glory

SHARI BRAND RAY

Bohannon Hall Press

Copyright © 2023 by Shari Brand Ray
All rights reserved.
Printed in the United States of America
First Edition

Illustrations © by Sarah Robin Coleman
Cover Art © by Sarah Robin Coleman

Library of Congress Control Number: 2023912127

Publisher's Cataloging-in-Publication Data

Ray, Shari Brand, 1960-
    Surprised by Glory: Essays on Searching for the Sublime/ by Shari Brand Ray ; illustrated by Sarah Robin Coleman.
    Niceville, FL: Bohannon Hall Press, 2023.
    270 p.: illustrations ; 23 cm.
    First edition.

1. Ray, Shari Brand—Literary collections. 2. Literary Collections—Essays. 3. Biography & Autobiography – Personal Memoirs. I. Title. II. Coleman, Sarah Robin, 1977-
PS3618.A9 S874 2023   2023912127

ISBN 979-8-9850298-7-1 (softcover)
ISBN 979-8-9850298-8-8 (hardcover)

Published by Bohannon Hall Press

To Lad and Rainey and Coleton and Teddy,
thank you for all the laughter
and all the back porch stories for all our lives

The glory of the moment is in the moment itself,
never in the moment to come.

Table of Contents

PROLOGUE	1
MORNINGS	7
SWIM COACHES	9
SCHOOLS	20
COMMERCIALS	25
ENEMIES	31
CHILDREN	45
IMPERFECTIONS	53
FOOTWEAR	61
STORMS	68
ANGELS	71
EVENINGS	87
NIGHT WATCHES	89
SYSTEMS	93
DREAD	105
SEDERS	111
COMFORTS	125
ACTIVE LOVE	133
OPHELIA	157
PAGEANTRIES	169
HOPE	177

AFTERNOONS — 185

TWO SKIES	187
ADVERSE CONDITIONS	194
LONELY	201
HOMES	209
FUNERALS I	224
FUNERALS II	231
ECLIPSE	239
DANCE	250

EPILOGUE — 263

ACKNOWLEDGEMENTS — 274

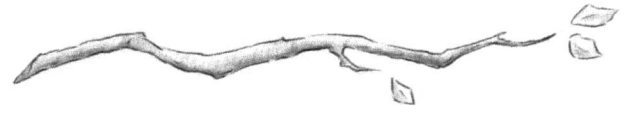

prologue

I am of the opinion that we normally find what we seek.

Earlier this year I went on a cruise with my mother to Japan. My mother spent four years in Japan as a child, where her father was stationed after World War II, and long had she longed to return, to revisit the memories of this vast and vivid part of her childhood. She wanted to see this lovely country again, in all its glory.

So, we went.

In the late afternoons after excursions and before dinner, I found myself standing on the deck of the ship or on the balcony of our stateroom for rather long periods of time just looking out over the vast expanse of water.

Seeing is about perspective, the lenses through which we choose to look at the world. From the middle of the Sea of Japan, no matter where I looked, the water surrounding the ship appeared the same—either all choppy or all smooth or all white-capping in a storm. From a 360-degree viewpoint with no land in sight, at any given moment the seawater looked exactly the same to me, for I am a novice at sea. I have not learned how to *see* the sea from anything beyond a surface level, I have not honed the skills to appreciate this water. But not so for an experienced sea captain. He knows the surface currents, understands the Coriolis effect on waves and tides, and identifies the wide variety of ocean movement, for he has studied these phenomena and knows what he sees. But for the average seafarer like me, the sea is the sea and where we are headed looks pretty much the same as where we've been. It's beautiful and vast, but that's about as far as I go, for I have not sought to know more about the sea.

One morning at dawn, about halfway through our cruise, dark storm clouds gathered thick and low above our ship, active in their rumble and swirl, and large, rolling waves accompanied the storm. I felt the ship shift under my feet and wondered what wonders such a dark day might bring. Then suddenly from the dense black middle of the storm clouds, a thin, straight, brilliant shaft of light beamed down onto the sea like a miracle, not far from the ship, and in that brief moment I saw the truth—this seawater is not the same at all! Rather, it is filled to the brim and overflowing with life! Below us, an enormous smack of jellyfish, perhaps a hundred or more, gathered at the edges of the slowing ship, flapping up and down in the tumult, and green-stippled mackerel leaped in twos and threes from the deep water into the singular bright light that danced in majesty atop the white-capping crowns of the stormy sea. The whole affair lasted but a moment, but I was there, witness to the glorious grandeur of this fine old Earth of ours.

prologue

As I said, I am of the opinion that we normally find what we seek. What I learn to see of the sea and the sky and the land and the people that inhabit this place depends on me and the lenses through which I look, my actual point of view, what I actively seek. So why waste my time pursuing anger, why indulge all this common fear and rage, why see only despair when I can choose to seek the *glory* that exists all around me? Or at least try.

Alas, there are many definitions for the word *glory* in the English language. As a noun, the word means 'honor or renown for notable achievements' and as an active verb it means 'to take great pride or pleasure in something.' But the Hebrew word for *glory*—תִּפְאֶרֶת—connotes 'heaviness or weight,' the magnificent weighty worth of a thing grand of substance and value, even to the point of splendor.

Moses asked God to show him His glory. And the Lord replied, 'I will cause all my goodness to pass in front of you... but you cannot see my face, for no one may see me and live.'

God continued, 'There is a place near me where you may stand on a rock. When my glory passes by, I will put you in a cleft in the rock and cover you with my hand until I have passed by. Then I will remove my hand and you will see my back, but my face must not be seen.'

So, what remains? What are we to seek from the cleft of the rock?

The high school seniors I teach often believe that a change in location will bring them the contentment they seek—they are *so* ready to go to college. But you and I know that a change of location doesn't alter things all that much, a new locale only changes where the peaceless heart tries (in vain) to get a good night's sleep. I contend that the pursuit of the sublime is a good place to start in our search for peace. So let us not idly think things will be easier at college or in another city or without a spouse or with *another* spouse or in a new job or whenever these darn kids finally grow up and get out on their own. The pursuit of glory is a practice, a finely-honed skill, and it begins in the familiar where we already live.

The search for God in the ordinary becomes a burning bush.

Or a thin shaft of light that brings sight to the blind. But we must avail ourselves of the possibility of a miracle.

I am of the opinion that we normally find what we seek. So why not seek after *glory,* for it is out there whether we choose to see it or not.

prologue

The writer Annie Dillard famously wrote, 'How we spend our days is, of course, how we spend our lives. What we do with this hour, and that one, is what we are doing.'

So, every day I must ask myself, what am I doing, accruing, rueing, pursuing with my limited number of wild and precious mornings, evenings, and afternoons? And how much of this activity is opening my eyes to glory, seeking splendor in the mundane, accepting the miraculous without logic or question, and laying down the spectacles of rage and hate that so easily beset us.

How I spend my days, of course, is how I spend my life, and I only have this one, so I will try to spend mine in pursuit of the sublime within the ordinary. I hope you will join me in the search. It's worth our best efforts.

mornings

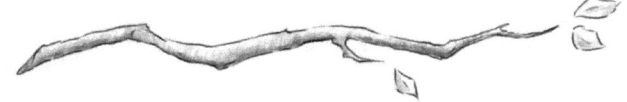

with gratitude for

swim coaches

> For whatever we lose (like a you or a me),
> It's always our self we find in the sea.
>
> e e cummings

My brother and I spent our childhood summers swimming at the Davis YMCA in Memphis. If you swam as a kid, or if you still swim, you never forget the acrid smell of chlorine lingering in the locker room and on your clothes after a full day of swimming. I still smell it occasionally, this unexpected delight, when I stand by a fountain or walk into a steamy locker room or even in an old, musty school-building before it's finally torn down. I smell it even now in the back seat of my car driving my tired grandson home from swimming at Miss Kim's pool.

If you ever loved swimming, you know you'll never forget, never want to forget the sharp aromas of a childhood spent at the local pool. The feeling of water in your ears. The smell of hamburgers grilling on a flat-top for the lunch crowd mingling with the starch-smell of chlorine on your skin and in your own hair. Nor do you ever forget the feeling of your red, swim-tired-yet-happy eyes and how good it feels to close them to rest, the chill of the air-conditioning in your mother's Buick, your wet skin all covered in shivers and your head lying hard against the back seat of a car heading home after a long practice, mother driving quiet.

I close my older eyes now and remember it all, just like that.

Once a person loves swimming she always will, I think, and even though I was not great at it, I dearly loved swimming on the swim team at the Davis Y. I came up through the ranks, taking all the lessons offered, summer after summer—Guppy, Fish, Flying Fish, Shark, Porpoise—finally finishing Life Guard training and joining the swim team. Swimming for Coach Furr. If memory serves at all, we were a great swim team, we won most of our meets most of the time. Cammie was the regional champion in breaststroke for several years in a row, unbeatable that one, and also number one in the city in the butterfly. No one could touch her in those years. Bart and Jamie were both all-state back-strokers and we had a record number of all-city swimmers. Bass was our best diver by (literally) leaps and bounds, he went all the way to Nationals once. Only our archenemies, the Mason Y swim team, could give us a run for our money in those days, and though those swimmers may remember it a bit differently, I'm quite sure the Davis Y won most of the time.

Without question, the Davis Y swim team prepared me for being a grownup. How could it not with the mighty

mornings

Coach Furr at the helm, with that backwoods Tennessee vernacular and his impeccable way with words, lessons a'plenty from his back pocket wisdom. Back then, none of us knew how politically incorrect he was, I'm not sure he knew. It was the way most of our men talked in those days, it was the early '70's in the South, at the edges of the Mississippi Delta, and we thought Coach Furr was hilarious. And wonderful.

All y'all are is a bunch of lazy bums today, every dang one of ya, he'd yell, throwing his blue Memphis State baseball cap down hard and splashy when we were lethargic and our times were slow. Do it again, again, he'd say. You ain't stoppin' 'til you droppin'. Keep this up and we'll lose to Mason this week for sure, Lord have mercy on all our wicked souls.

And so, we swam. We gave our best, for him.

In those days, the old men spoke another language. You boys are swimmin' like women, Coach Furr said, the deepest cut of all, and the boy-bashing brought us girls to hilarious tears every time, and not understanding that the bashing was ostensibly two-sided, we howled with laughter at our male counterparts who promptly starting swimming with every ounce of fortitude they had left, even after far too many laps. Gloria Steinem would have made her way to Memphis for sure if she'd had any idea what was going on down here, but like I said, most of our old men talked like this back then, and we saw no harm in it at the time.

In the summer of my eleventh year, I spent far too much time fancying the idea that being a guy was cooler than being a girl. It looked to me like the guys had more fun, what with all the strutting and the constant bodily noises and the genesis of the well-placed cuss word into a regular simple sentence. Even the way the boys exited the pool was remarkable to me, fantastic. All of our older team guys, the fifteen- and sixteen-year-olds, jumped out of the water in the same fashion; in this one big splashy *swoosh*, they could push their upper bodies into the air with their muscle-y arms and land one-footed on the pool deck like they were born doing it. Then, if that wasn't enough, they brought their strong bodies to full height while shaking their shaggy heads the whole time like giant wet pups and adjusting their Speedos to out-of-water propriety and then spit with great confidence right onto the pool deck, all in one grand fluid movement that was to me a perfection Poseidon himself must surely envy. I wanted to be able to do that like I'd never wanted to do anything else. So, I practiced. I gave this pool-exiting movement far more time and energy than I gave my breaststroke, that's for sure, but not only did I not master the great *swoosh* no matter how hard I tried, my pool exit remained a sort of flop, a true belly-flop onto the deck with skinny arms flailing and skinny legs dangling at awkward angles in the water. Despite my constant attention that summer, my pool exit evolved into more of forward-roll-push-up-stomach-scraping combination, a grand exercise of grimacing and grunting and tugging, like a lobster hatchling trying to pull her awkward way up a concrete wall.

That's a cool pool exit you've got there, said no one to me, ever.

What I could accomplish though, upon finally crawling out of the water, was the head-shaking and the spitting. Now *that* I could do, for I had much hair then, and I shook those long, black, preteen curls so hard I felt a bit of nausea and a touch of vertigo, at which point I cocked my drying head back as far as my little neck allowed then slung the whole business forward in a dark blur of speed and let one fly—I spit. And I discovered that I was great at spitting. My brother and I practiced in the back yard and I could spit as far and with as much vigor as any eleven-year-old in the Volunteer State. It was a sight to behold, I must admit. (I considered contacting the Guinness Book of World Records, but for some reason my mother discouraged that thought.) What I lacked in upper arm strength I made up for in spittle and sheer tongue-power. I practiced hard and then I executed, *Ptooey!*, and the result was worth all my effort.

Coach Furr watched my dandy performance only a time or two before he made his way over to the girls' bench. Miss Brand, may I speak with you? Coach Furr smiled politely. Sure, I squeaked, for I knew my time had finally come round at last. He'd seen my work, knew I was brimming full of the right stuff, and I wondered if he was going to promote me to the breaststroke leg of the girls' relay team against Mason Y in the weekend meet. I wondered if the Olympics had called and needed me to sub for Mark Spitz. I wondered if he'd noticed my impressive pool-exiting-hair-tossing-reared-back-spitting extravaganza.

Turns out, he had.

Miss Brand, I appreciate your hard work these days, especially on your breast-stroke, and I want you to know it has not gone unnoticed. You are improving every day and I'm very proud of you. Keep it up. But I want to tell something and I don't want you to forget it. He leaned in and I knew this was a moment for my eager, burning ears only, Coach was talking only to me. This was unprecedented. Don't waste all your time spitting and practicing at spitting, he said. You are a fine swimmer and a good girl, and spitting won't add to the specialness of who you already are. Be yourself, not someone else, and that will always be enough. Winking, he patted me gently on the head and I knew we were done.

Thus concluded the last days of my spitting. Some spectacles are simply not worth the effort. I figure most aren't.

So far, I have failed to mention a most important fact about my aquatic career, perhaps *the* most important: I never won a race, not a single one. I'm not sure I was ever on a winning relay team, and upon consideration and a quick glance into the rearview mirror, I realize Coach Furr most certainly placed all of the weakest swimmers on relay teams together, saving the stronger swimmers to relay against the Mason Y, giving the Davis Y an actual chance to win the meet. I never thought about this until right now, sitting on my back porch like a contented old lady watching the humming birds in their migration south, and I suppose that's because Coach Furr never made me feel like a weak swimmer. Not one time. In fact, as I said earlier, I thought about the Olympics more than once, which I also mentioned to my mother, who listened politely like she always does.

For one, I had no natural talent for athletics, not really. Stamina, yes, and as far as perseverance is concerned, my mother insisted on our flexing our muscles and building up the ability to 'stick with' something, being old-school and all and no fan of quitters. I have inherited this from her, it's in our blood. But natural swimming talent, or athletic prowess of any kind for that matter, is not our family's DNA, so no matter how hard I worked, my talents in the pool were limited. In part because of my left hand. Born with a short arm and only three stiff fingers on my left hand, my strokes were out of balance, my right side so much stronger than my weaker, thinner left. And since I couldn't cup my little hand at all, pool-water simply flowed through those three fixed fingers like a sieve, thus I simply had less leverage to pull myself through the water. It's a wonder, I suppose, that I didn't eventually just begin swimming in circles, ever leaning to my stronger right side. Oh, there was a bit of kind chatter for a moment about a little plastic prosthetic for me to wear while competing, but nothing ever came of it.

Anyway, there's something important about learning at an early age that we cannot and will not win at everything we do, no matter how much we love it or how hard we try.

And so, the good swimming season of my eleventh summer ended right before school started back in September, as all good things must, with a family cookout and the Awards Night where Coach Furr handed out the trophies and awards. These were the '70s, long before everyone on the team received a trophy for participating, so most of us weak-to-plain-old-regular swimmers just sat at our table and ate grilled hamburgers and chips and ice cream and cheered for the same names who always won because we understood they were the best swimmers and deserving of trophies and I guess we just considered that fact fair-and-square. Cammie was the state breast-stroker and deserving of an award, as was Bass the state diving champ and Bart and Jamie and the others on the relay team who swam so well at the meet where

There's something important about learning at an early age that we cannot and will not win at everything we do.

we trampled the Mason Y, and we regular swimmers knew we had absolutely nothing to do with that stunning victory. It was the same every year, and in my memory, we cheered and cheered, just glad I suppose to be a part of a winning team and to sit together at sticky tables and eat Nutty Buddy ice cream cones on a hot, end-of-summer night.

Imagine our surprise when Coach Furr picked up the megaphone at the tail end of Awards Night and announced, in his squawking megaphone coach-voice, a new award this year, a trophy for the Most Improved swimmer. This total break of Awards Night protocol shook us all like a tremor from the New Madrid fault. We weaker swimmers, eyes now wide and giddy with wonder like children at Christmas, grinned at the possibility of the miraculous, imagined for a single breath hearing a name other than the oft-called names of the greats, hearing *our own name* come out of Coach Furr's mouth. We weren't sure we believed it could happen, or even that it should.

Last summer I sat at Miss Kim's pool watching my grandson swim when I heard a murmuring float over those chlorinated waters, a whisper from the winds that Coach Furr had died. I found his obituary online and was more than surprised to find that his lovely obituary said nothing about Coach Furr ever coaching the swim team at the Davis Y. Not one word.

He was my mother's age when he died. He left behind children and a bereaved wife.

I owe a great deal of my self-confidence and so many happy childhood memories to the Davis YMCA swim team and Coach Fred Furr in particular. It turns out some people really are good-hearted, which is good news.

When we moved my mother to her retirement community, I found the trophy—Most Improved Swimmer—the only trophy I ever won.

Thanks, Coach.

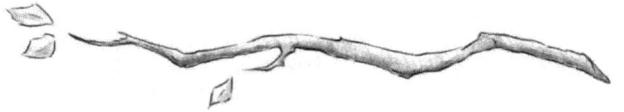

in appreciation for

schools

Instruction does much, but encouragement everything.
Goethe

Back to school is a hopeful place. Clutches of pointy pencils newly-sharpened, unlined journals clean and at the ready, desks wiped down, the slight pungent scent of Clorox hovering in the expectant air. Book bags, asleep under messy summer beds, now shaken out and dusted off and standing at attention near brand-new lunch boxes and freshly-pressed uniform skirts. Summer reading almost complete, dog-eared pages full of lines too beautiful to be forgotten. And names printed neatly on everything, in permanent marker.

I am always ready for school to start again.

My room is tidy, syllabus ready. The day before school starts, early in the morning, I stand in my classroom with a hot coffee in hand and listen to the silence, knowing full well this is the last time these hallowed halls will be quiet for months. I already hear the echoes of girlish laughter wafting up the stairway, making its way into the fibers of the carpet, and into the beams and rafters of the place.

mornings

They are coming, they are here.

Students have been in the hallway now most of the morning, clinking and clanging their books into nice rows in their lockers, the first and last time any of these books will enjoy such order. A father helps his freshman daughter learn to use a combination lock for the first time, their heads bent together over the stubborn digits, their concentration joint, and thick. I wonder as I watch if this father isn't taking more time than necessary teaching his daughter this new skill, lingering in the pleasure of a lovely moment that he is wise enough to know will never come again.

I meet these people, parents of students who may not be mine for another two or three years. I'm the *senior* English teacher, I say again and again, but these parents introduce their fourteen-year-old to me anyway, tell me snippets of her story, what's she has done all summer and how much she loves to read and they ask me if I know she is a dancer. Girls glance shyly over their shoulders at our talking, wondering if they should be embarrassed or pleased by such conversation. I smile and wink to let them know that all is well.

I stand for a few minutes in the freshman hallway. Even in the excitement and noise of this chaotic moment, seventy freshman girls and their parents all in one hallway at the same time, clutching books and journals and backpacks and calculators, I can hear the tune of an old song hovering above the din. I hear it every year and sang it myself when I stood in their shoes, of watching my child cross the tremulous and glorious threshold from child to teen. It's the song of growing up, of going to high school, of growing older, and watching our children do the same.

So many fears haunt the notes and lyrics of this old melody. Fears birthed, perhaps, as we stood on this threshold ourselves so many years back, wondering what was waiting for us on the banks of this unknown shore. And now a child of our own stands on the selfsame shore and all the roles have changed, everyone seeking firm footing on shifting sands.

The lockers on the freshman hall echo the melody this morning. The old lockers listen as new people arrive on the hall and they smile as we all hear the old words wafting yet again up the school stairs. New kids, new parents, but always the same lyrics, the same song, the tone of which is mixed in a haunting melody of joy laced in quiet undertones of doubt: is she ready, am I? Is she smart enough, prepared enough? Has she done her work well, have I? What unexpected trial lurks around some dark corner I didn't even know existed?

Will she remember not to get in cars with strangers? Did she eat a good breakfast? Will she bring her books to class? Will people be nice to her? And more importantly, will she be nice to them?

I know this anxious song, have heard it countless times with young ears and old. But I remember what these folks may have forgotten on this exciting day of moving in and moving up. Someone is here all day long, waiting to help her, ready.

Her teacher.

To be a good teacher, a really good one, I must remember one essential thing every day, the most significant aspect of all. Not the iambic pentameter of a sonnet or a certain chemical equation or irregular French verbs, as important as those things are. I must remember that my student is a human being, and someone's child. And I must treat each of my students as I would want someone to treat my own child. Not as a number or a disruption or a form or a type, but as a human being that God purposefully placed in my path, someone special placed under my tutelage for a few brief months, a person who will change and transform under my instruction, hopefully for the better, although this choice is hers.

Someone who may be under a terrible strain away from school, a fact I must remember when her face is long or bitter or silent or uncooperative or sleepy. Someone who may remember me as kind and helpful, someone who made her life better, easier, richer—this simply must be the case. Each student who crosses a new threshold into a new classroom this school year deserves this chance, the chance to be loved and accepted and well-taught. There is simply no other alternative, there cannot be.

The freshmen are chattering, squealing and giggling and I am thankful that happiness is noisy.

Each day as I walk this hallway and cross the threshold of my room to teach another group of girls, I will adjust my glasses and remind myself to see this, to really see it. Then I will remind myself that each one of my students is someone's daughter, and I will treat her as I want people to treat my child. And my grandson in his first-grade classroom just down the road. I will do my best, for this is a fine way to try to live a good life.

with caution for

commercials

Life ain't fair.
Everybody

When we were little, my brother and I loved to go grocery shopping with our mother. Fred Montesi's was my mother's supermarket of choice in those days, this Memphis staple with her vast variety of culinary neighborhoods destined to lure small children beyond the barriers of civilization into the realm of raw, primitive, barbaric desire. And every other week Montesi's was the highlight of our lives, for we were introduced to the existential phenomenon of human choice in all its guts and glory.

The cereal row alone with its agonizing predicament of choice, Cap'n Crunch or Quisp or Quake or Apple Jacks, each and all singing their peculiar siren song to children ages five-to-nine, tempting the young with promises no mortal dare boast, teasing innocent children, like my brother and me, who watch too many commercials on TV and whose mother can afford only one box per kid to last for the next two weeks, of the glories far beyond our ken.

Sometimes my mother pushes one cart and pulls the other herself while my brother and I play and dream in the potato chip aisle.

Life ain't fair.

And the frozen food section with her frozen hashbrown potatoes, those hard bricks of promise which we will soon smother in a bath of Heinz ketchup, are finer than the ambrosia of any god anywhere. Aisle after aisle of endless culinary possibilities become almost more than my brother and I can bear. Every two weeks my mother fills two grocery carts to the brim in order to feed her hungry family of four. She pushes one cart and I the other, although sometimes my mother pushes one and pulls the other herself while my brother and I play and dream in the potato chip aisle. Brother sometimes sits underneath the cart beside the rattly wheels, the days of fancy grocery carts that look like cars in a distant future far, far away.

Life ain't fair.

And oh, the candy counter, the scene of my first misdemeanor. I sneak a Brach's butterscotch from the glistening heap of gold at the store front (my mother consistently forbade any indulgence which included this big rock candy mountain), unwrap the precious treasure and pop the sugary-thing right into my mouth without a thought until, just seconds later, my sticky lips betray me and my mother sees the guilty standing before her, caught red-handed, and without delay marches me to stand trial before the tribunal of the store manager and his two grinning assistants—not a jury of *my* peers, I'd like you to know—where I am found guilty of my crime, and while immediately forgiven by the management, the punishment for my crime is nothing less than spitting out the candy at once and borrowing pennies from the cavernous depths of my mother's brown purse to pay the price for my misdeed, pennies that I will then work off at home on the chain gang of extra chores. In abject humiliation I walk three silent steps behind my mother while my brother gets to choose *both* boxes of cereal for our two-week allotment.

Life ain't fair.

There was not a great deal of money in the Brand family in those days, so if memory serves, my brother and I would each get to choose *one* item for ourselves, every other week. A nearly paralyzing decision, its import so incalculable we do not want to mess this up, for it will be a fortnight before we have another opportunity. I don't remember what I chose the week about which I'm writing, but I do remember my brother's choice, Pillsbury crescent dinner rolls. An odd choice for a preschooler perhaps, but why not? As I scamper down aisles of cookies and pies and jellies in search of my bi-weekly prize, Mother checks and double-checks my brother's decision, but undaunted that little guy was (and still is) standing firm in the confidence of his five years. Pillsbury crescent rolls seem written in his stars. He wants to have them for dinner this very night.

mornings

Back at our house, we help Mama take the groceries in and help unload them from their sacks and put up the pantry items in good order while she wipes out the refrigerator before putting the new items in. She cracks the whip, that one, always wiping down the fridge before restocking. These slow minutes tick by in tedium, waiting, waiting for Mama to finish so that we can open our store goodies. Brother's Pillsbury crescent rolls stand tall and lean like a tower, at-the-ready beside the hamburger meat and spaghetti sauce, a regular night's menu for four.

I want to open the rolls now now now! Brother shouts when the last of the groceries are finally put up and the brown paper sacks are folded and stored on the floor of the pantry. Time to start supper.

All right then, Mama says with a grin, and she kneels to show Brother how to pull the paper from around the cannister and then pound the tube on the side of the counter…

I know how to do it, I've seen it on TV! Brother shouts in full voice, rich in excitement. Mother helps Brother take the paper off anyway, and he pounds the tube of crescent rolls against the counter in great fervor, as seen in the commercial. After a couple of good, hard, concentrated whacks, the tube of dough dutifully opens at its seam with its signature *whoosh* and reveals the gooeyness inside. Success, Mother says with a smile, but it is instantly evident that Brother feels no such emotion.

With neither word nor movement, the sun stands still for a few seconds as my brother stares unbelieving at the dough, then back to Mother, then back to the tube in his hand before he breaks into heart-wrenching five-year-old tears and flings himself down, down, down to the kitchen floor in the agony of his despair.

What's the matter, baby-boy? Mama consoles, kneeling at his side. Why are you crying?

Where's the Dough Boy? my brother wails, the Dough Boy is supposed to jump out and let me poke him in the belly, he giggles when you poke him in the belly. Where's the Dough Boy, where's the Dough Boy? Like on TV!

Oh, dear Brother. One of us failed to tell five-year-old you that not everything we hear and see and sing and read and trust is real, although our imaginations so often tell us something to the contrary. Sometimes there is disappointment here. Not everything we see on TV is true.

After a weepy, quiet supper, Mother made chocolate chip cookies. They tasted sweet, and warm. Sometimes sweet and warm has to be enough.

Because, well, life ain't fair.

aware of

enemies

> Whenever you are confronted with an opponent,
> conquer him with love.
> Gandhi

There is drama in the pecking order of things. Each morning I watch a spectacle at the bird feeder in my yard, a tragicomedy of great pith and moment on a stage where one's station is not only defined but that definition accepted without question. Nature works like that, her order is unyielding.

Birds of all types visit my small side yard. They storm all aflutter the moment I bring out the seed, helping themselves to easy food at the metal feeder hanging under the eave of my roof. The birds are not afraid of me. I show up most days, so they are accustomed. They wait in branches for the few seconds it takes me to fill the feeder, then race to the seed the moment the screen door slams behind me.

The plentiful sparrows arrive first, dancing about for a place to perch. They do not fight much. Some gather on the ground below, waiting for the seeds that fall, others find a place on the ledge of the feeder even as it swings in the breezes of each season, but there is little fussing. These sparrows understand the nature of abundance, I buy birdseed in bulk.

The doves understand this less. I hear them before I see them, their cooing precedes their coming. I see them from my chair on the back porch, they perch on my neighbor's angled roof and plot their attack strategies.

Doves are bigger and heavier than house sparrows. The average house sparrow weighs around an ounce, barely heavier than a feather, while the average dove weighs around five ounces and is almost double in length to a sparrow. Time comes, as it always does, for a dove to invade the territory. She flies from her perch and lands heavy on the feeder, scattering both sparrows and seeds. The dove eats what she will when she will, and the sparrows stay below, taking what the dove scatters, waiting.

Cardinals arrive in their fire-engine-fury and shoo the doves away, pushy birds these red ones. The doves flee the cardinals as they must, but not without proper protest, though their angry high-pitched cooing proves fruitless. The doves will stay and feed until some predator comes for them. This is the way of the world.

The blue jay arrives in the grandeur of his blue-and-white-crestedness, his royal plumed head turned tall in all its finery, that bragger. No bird seems prepared to stand up to him, none as beautiful or majestic, not at my feeder anyway.

mornings

Each act of this drama brings a species of bird weightier and grander than the one before. As long as there is no crow or squirrel in the neighborhood, the blue jay stays the longest, eating his fill. Soon enough, though, every bird grows bored or the food runs out, and eventually they all fly away to other feeders, greener pastures, better seed selection.

Except the sparrows.

All along, throughout the entire parade of bigger bully-birds in all their brute beauty and threat, the sparrows have waited, some in hiding, but most standing just offstage, in the wings—on the ground, in the bushes, in the trees. They sit and watch and wait for their cue. When the bigger birds fill up and move on to grander climes, the house sparrows return to the feeder, as if being overpowered by one stronger is of no consequence at all. As if it never happened. Accustomed to this pecking order, they seem to be at peace with it. I refill the feeder and scoot out of the way. The sparrows offer no thanks for this abundance, but I am privy to their daily song and the chittering and clicking of their feeding, which is thanks enough.

This pecking order is sometimes difficult to watch, though, its ugly pushiness often seems more of a disorder to me. Large shoves small, prettier trumps plainer, strong pecks at weak; it is survival of the fittest out there, just under the eave of my roof. Bullies make demands, they want what they want when they want and they push until they get it. I ask the sparrows how they live and feed with such peace of mind, but they do not answer.

If I'm not careful, I can forget about the sparrows in the winter. Most common house sparrows do not migrate when the cold comes, especially here in West Tennessee where the winters are mild, relatively speaking, so these sparrows stick around. I don't know where they roost or where their song is in the cold months, but they are here nonetheless. I think of them in the winter and rise from the sleepy warmth of my couch to give them a bit of seed, but it's more sporadic, I'm afraid. They fend for themselves on cold, dark days. Yet they neither toil nor spin, no worry seems to invade their patient chirping. They do not even scold my tardiness.

Where are your bullies now, sparrows? Do they push you from your feeder and steal your seed in winter like they do in summer? Seldom does a cardinal or blue jay show up to the feeder in the cold, nor doves, nor crows. Even the pesky squirrel stays away, munching somewhere on buried acorns, or asleep.

Sparrow, are you bullied in the quiet of winter? Do your enemies ever just go away? I need to know because I have a personal stake in this game. I have enemies as well.

One day an enemy-bird flies up unannounced to the feeder

where I feed, where I've been spending my long days and years in what I thought was relative safety, munching on seed and soaking up a little sun. Reading a book, writing a story or two. I do not see this enemy coming, for until now I have sensed no need to be watching my back. I think she has been perched on my neighbor's roof for a while, planning her attack, but I cannot be sure.

What surprises me most is the ease of her assault, the sheer speed of it, like an aggressive blue jay swooping in amongst the simple sparrows. *Whoosh.* One phone call, one poorly written email or a letter not written at all seems to be all it takes to acquire an enemy these days, one misunderstanding and all communication breaks down entirely. I guess it has always been that simple, but I don't know for sure. I should have seen this coming, though, I read books—Othello has his Iago, David his Saul. Still, it is a great shock to my system, I must say, as I have been oblivious to enemy activity in my garden for so many of my days.

Enemies are for *other* people, I think and thought. But everyone's hour comes round at last, the poet says. My enemy-bird arrives and she is hungry and demanding and pushing and pecking, and I realize how unprepared I am for this attack. I have no weapon honed for such an assault, no quiver from which to pull a ready arrow, not a single bow in sight.

How should I then live?

Perhaps I should try the tactics of the sparrow, flitting here and yon and staying out of the way, low to the ground, just trying to wait it out unseen in the shadows. But this doesn't always work well. My enemy pokes and prods, talks behind my back and tries to flush me out of my hiding places. Maybe I should try acting like a dove when the cardinal arrives, shaking my thin claw in protest, trying to have my story heard.

Listen to me, there is another story here, another side to things, I squeak and squawk. But to no avail. No one hears my song and my enemy does not care. She is stronger and more colorful and her squawk is louder and she has more energy than I can muster.

I have no wings prepared for such a battle.

I try one more tactic, a human one this time. I try to reason with the enemy-bird, try to listen with empathy, tell her my side, try to smooth things over and find a peaceful branch where we both can perch, or at least a common tree. Yet everything I do makes things worse. I speak kind words, she condemns me for platitudes; I write a bereavement note, she judges the authenticity and flies away angrier than before, and then I realize fully, for the first time in my life, that I am no peacekeeper, and worse, neither am I peacemaker, as I was so sure I was.

Humans are not sparrows and I am no god to fix this universe.

mornings

I watch the sparrows at the feeder as I write this, munching in the calm quiet of their common table. Friends they are, companions eating, no fear, no fighting. Even the bit of rain that begins to fall does not disrupt their feast, they shake their collective feathers dry. But the enemy-dove perches still, relentless on the neighbor's roof, ready to pounce and steal. The smaller birds must know she's there for this happens every single day. And still they flit in peacefulness at the feeder.

I have questions for the sparrows.

What is your secret, little ones? How such peace in constant adversity? I steal over to the thin screen that separates us, and I get as close as I can with these many questions on my lips. With your enemy always at the ready, what is the secret to your peace? I ask. A small bird cocks her head to the left and chirps out her answer, and for the first time, I understand her song: we sparrows are wise, the little bird sings, because we acknowledge that enemies behave like enemies.

Sparrows recognize an enemy and that she is near; they are not surprised by this truth as I am, my grand mistake—how could *I* possibly have enemies, what with my being so nice and all?

37

But there is more. A secret to understanding antagonism has to do with expectations. These wise sparrows do not expect friendly behavior from their enemies. They know the dove and the blue jay and the squirrel are *not friends*, they know predators will swoop and steal, this is what they do, and the sparrows have a plan in place for an attack—they get out of the way. They skitter fast and find a safe bush or high tree limb and perch, maybe even a very long while, and wait for their adversary to wear herself out and go. They are neither surprised nor offended when the cardinal eats all their seed, for they know an enemy takes what she wants. Such is her nature.

It's clearer in the natural world, I think, at least the lines are cleaner. A predator is ever a predator. A bear will eat a fish every time, it's out of balance if a dog doesn't chase a cat, or a cat a mouse. Animals do not expect an enemy to act like a friend—this is their wisdom.

The system must be the same in our civilized world (if there is such a thing). I've gotten off track a time or two and stumbled into sadness because of faulty expectations; expecting a person who is clearly behaving like an enemy to all-of-a-sudden begin acting like a friend. Such absurd thinking. That's not to say there's no room for growth and movement and even forgiveness in any situation, grace and forgiveness being ultimate goals in human relations. Of course.

But getting anywhere close to this goal requires seeing things as they are. I must ask myself reasonable questions: is my enemy trustworthy in her dealings with me? No. Is she leaning in to make the situation better? No. Is she listening to me, at all? No.

Is she only able to see the situation through her own lens? Yes.

And foolishly I think my enemy will ask these questions of me. But I have learned that predators rarely ask questions.

To have an enemy in one's life is hard enough, but to have expectations of kindness or grace from an enemy can drive one mad. The choice to change is my own. Waiting for an adversary to change is like expecting a hawk to be gentle with a field mouse.

Once in my reading I came across this doozy in Matthew 5, 'But I say unto you, Love your enemies, bless them that curse you, do good to them that hate you, and pray for them...' What, pray for your enemies? Love them? Bless them that curse you and do good to them? What does this even mean?

I teach at a lovely Episcopal school where we have chapel every day, and at the end of each service, we kneel to say the school prayer. This act of kneeling is an important practice for me, a quiet act of praise, a time to pause, to bend.

Kneeling this day, I forfeit the school prayer and ponder

instead Saint Matthew's idea, Do good to your enemies. I wonder how can I do this, I am estranged from my enemy. How can I love my enemy when I do not even see her? I only hear of the cruel words and jibes that remain, floating aloft in the constant sky and the crashing, never-ceasing waves of social media.

Sometimes, though, I can hear whispers blowing around in the stillness.

This day in chapel, I hear God in a quiet voice that sounds like young girls praying, chanting a school prayer—'Almighty God, Fountain of all wisdom, be with us, we pray Thee, in our work today...'

Look to your left, the Voice prompts, so I look. Beside me, across the aisle, sit the sixth-grade girls, the littlest among us. Heads bowed, fingers laced, they kneel to pray, and I see the moving of lips and collective reverence. I hear God's voice, but more, I feel it in my soul, deep deep down saying, Love the children. You can love your enemy by loving her children. If you cannot yet pray for your enemy, if you cannot do good to her because she will not let you or you simply do not want to, then begin by praying for her children. Practice paradox, do what an enemy would not do.

I bend my tired back, try to relax my wounded shoulders, open my mouth in faith and hope for words to come.

mornings

Words often precede feeling, actions as well. I pray for the children of my enemy. Words cross my lips and I soften, a little. The children, Christ reminds me, the kingdom of God is made up of such as these.

When cruel words resurface, as cruel words will, I bend and pray for the children of the slanderer, my enemy.

When hate overwhelms and consumes, I bend and pray for the children, that love will permeate their lives and the adult's anger will find no home in them.

Where I cannot accomplish peace, I bend and pray the children will develop peaceful relationships, honest conversations. I pray for their protection from the anxiety that hate engenders. I pray for love, for them and for me.

When I taste the cruelty and relentlessness of my enemy, when I am reminded of this bitterness and taste it afresh on the tongue, then I bend and pray for her children. It is a start.

'Fear not, therefore; you are of more value than the sparrows,' says Saint Matthew.

David, Israel's greatest king, had a most logical solution when his turn with the enemy came around; like my sparrows, David hid, he took to the caves. His angry enemy was the current king, and when this King Saul pursued him, simmering and slandering and chunking spears in jealous rages at the young musician, David ran to the caves and lived as a fugitive for many years and simply waited Saul out. Now this David was no weakling, mind you. He was a giant-slayer and the mightiest of warriors in his own right—'David has killed tens of thousands' was the glad song sung by the adoring crowds upon David's victorious return from battle.

The mighty warriors of David's army begged him to lash out against the bully Saul; throw spears back, destroy the enemy, give him a taste of his own medicine. Logical advice, for another man perhaps. But wise David did just the opposite. He saw his enemy realistically—hurtful, unpredictable, and reckless—and left Saul alone to wallow in his own angry choices.

David left Saul alone with God. 'Vengeance is mine,' sayeth the Lord. Time and God will take care of this, David decides, it is out of my hands. So, David hunkered down in the darkness with a friend or two or three and his music and his God and waited Saul out. He chose a healthier path than lashing back at an out-of-control enemy. He could have easily killed Saul a multitude of times but he never did, never considered it, really. He didn't toil, neither did he spin, and both God and time took care of the rest.

Saul died and David's hands remained clean.

A chicken will behave like a chicken, clucking and scratching, a dog will bark and dig, a cat will purr and lick, to expect anything other borders on the absurd. An enemy will behave

mornings

like an enemy, thus, expecting her to behave like a friend is nonsense. My sparrows and King David are far more reasonable than I.

The little birds chirp anew at the feeder, another song, a new message.

We sparrows are wise because we understand a most important law of nature, and it is this: find your fellow sparrows to fly through this land with, you don't need all that many.

Flee and hide together when the blue jays show up. The bushes will protect us and if not, we know where there are some nice caves, we led King David to them in his day. We will all wait it out together. God sees us there, too.

Nestle up close and remind the other sparrows of the seed in abundance at this feeder, even when you must wait a bit until the bullies clear. Perch with your friends, the few real ones, and sing to the One who feeds for it gives him pleasure to answer and to provide more than you could even imagine. He always gives more than is necessary, and the feeder-woman buys her birdseed in bulk, so eat up! There's plenty where that comes from.

Sometimes, after all is eaten, they congregate in a tidy row on the wooden railing and chirp at me as if to say, Wake up, feeder-woman, we are out of food again. I hear their cry and bring more food. Why should I not, for I have much seed to give, far more than they could ever think or dream. My birds feast on feed they did not produce and eat seeds they did not harvest. I do too, and like me, the birds eat in abundance from a repast they did not earn. They hover over the empty feeding-table, they know where and from whom the seeds come. What they do not know, cannot understand, is the greatest pleasure of this process is for me, the giver, and that their constant return to the feeder is the giver's delight, thanks enough.

A grand paradox exists in the heavens—the One who provides the seed also allows the enemy. But why? Because he loves my enemy as much as he loves me, all his children are precious in his sight, no matter their track record. Everyone is offered a second chance in this kingdom. This is part of the mystery of living on this blighted star, a love that logic cannot tolerate. God gives and he protects; in him, there is always enough of both, no matter what it might look like on a particularly rainy day when all the seeds fall from the feeder and wash into the unforgiving mud or the afternoon when it seems the bully-enemy will never fly away. The sparrow feeds in the constant faith of her Father's care. What need hath she to toil or spin.

My sparrows fly unfettered because they remember from where the seed comes. At the moment, there is not a blue jay in sight.

remembering the

children

The soul is healed by being with children.
Fyodor Dostoyevsky

For my grandson Teddy and all my students, past and present and old and young.

Perhaps my favorite song to sing in chapel at St. Mary's, my school, is 'The Servant Song.' Teddy, I will teach it to you soon, maybe one afternoon on a walk over to the big dirt hill or as we walk around by the lake at Shelby Farms, and we will sing it together as loud as we want and as many times as we like and never stop singing it until our voices grow tired and it's time to sleep. Here is my favorite stanza, it makes me think of you every time:

We are pilgrims on the journey
We are brothers on the road
We are here to help each other
Walk the mile and bear the load.

We are created to walk alongside one another, pilgrims on this grandest of journeys. How kind of God to put us here together, at the same time in the same place! Of all the billions of folk whose feet have already touched the miraculous soil of this remarkable planet and for the billions yet to come, I get to walk my time together with you, and this is such a fine thing that it takes my breath away. I think of it all day long.

Perhaps the most important thing to know about being here is that you are not alone. I think you already know this, deep in your bones, don't you, Teddy? That's why you wanted your mama to sit beside you when you played in your pirate tent in the old house and why you stood by your daddy in the yard when you both raked the leaves even though you were too little to do anything more than simply stir the leaves around, unpiling your daddy's piles. Try to remember this precious gift, the fact that you are not alone, for this may be the most precious gift of all.

It's important to have someone older to walk along with, someone to protect you a bit and teach you a few things like kindness and humor and how to look before you cross the street and grammar and punctuality and the value of money and that we always treat people well no matter who they are, no matter what. To read all the books we can and to keep you from getting too close to the fire. I'm so glad to be walking alongside you in this life—it's a great gift.

But perhaps the converse is even truer, though, maybe it's even more important to have someone younger to walk with, someone to remind me that this rock dusted with shiny mica and this stick bent like a crooked elbow and this glorious yellow dandelion weed growing right up through the concrete (yes, this very one!) are not only a good part of the walk but the most important part, for the young still see the awed beauty of each natural phenomenon through unjaded, less anxious, more honest lenses, while the older of us too often don spectacles aimed toward the blue glow of a 24-hour news cycle.

Someone to remind me that I can stand again after falling off a scooter, even if I only have one person to help me back up and that sometimes, in the best of times, there is more than one person to help me back up, and that's one of the loveliest of experiences of all in this life. Oh, and someone to remind me that it's always always always OK to cry.

I sometimes wonder if it is tiresome for you and for all the children, forever teaching us grownups things we should already know, things we should be teaching *you*, like forgiveness is actually easier than it sounds, especially when I recall all the mistakes I've made. And that lying silent on the grass by the lake at Shelby Farms watching the clouds float by is one of the purest forms of praise. And that being kind to animals and patient with little children, even when they ask the same question two thousand times in a row, is what Jesus would do—what Jesus *did* do when he drew the children to himself.

I hope you will not grow too weary in your tutelage of me, for I still have so much to learn. And please know I'm listening, even when I fall asleep while I'm reading you books.

But there are a few things I want to tell you, some differences between you and me, the young and the old. I think these are true, for the most part.

1

When we are young, we explore, and when we are old, we reflect.

So go forth and explore everything and sing as loud as you want and don't worry what the scowling older ladies walking by think, even if they *shush* you, because their generational crabbiness is their choice and has nothing to do with you. Kick over all the rocks you find so you can see what magic lies just underneath the surface and I'll bring a pencil and write it all down so we won't forget. Oh, and remember I have extra-large pockets in my jacket made especially for autumn leaf-collecting. And rocks.

The philosopher Soren Kierkegaard said that while life is lived forwards, it can only be understood backwards, and I agree.

2

When we are young, we seek justice, and when we are old, we seek mercy.

You go to school now and play hard on the playground every day, it's your favorite part of the day, except for maybe music and math and iLab and reading and journal time and story time and chicken-nugget-day in the lunch room. I wish you could stay there forever. But people will eventually tell you it's a jungle out there, and while there's truth in that statement, the bigger truth is that what We the People actually want is equity, we want what is fair. And when we are not treated fairly, we want justice, and we want it right now (as a group, we humans are an impatient breed). Now, the pursuit of justice is a mighty good thing, but like all good things, there can be an ugly underbelly to it as well. It can be cruel and heartless, and left untreated and unchecked, what is cruel and heartless evolves into a monster, never into art, or a flower.

When you are older, you will know how you've been wounded, but you will also know how you have wounded. A wise man, which you will be, will then start to see the beauty in mercy, perhaps more than justice. The strongest of us work to develop a nice balance of justice and mercy in our lives. But when you find yourself stuck between the hardness of justice and the softness of mercy, choose mercy. Always choose mercy.

President Abraham Lincoln said that he found that mercy bears richer fruit than strict justice, and I agree with him too.

3

When we are young, we grow prickly, and when we are old, we grow soft.

The young will often fight and choose to alienate on principle, for they are out to save the world and that's not a bad thing because this old world could use some saving. For what is the purpose of fire, if not to burn? But the old know the world is also saved one kindness at a time, one gentleness at a time, loving one broken person at a time.

The poet Henry Wadsworth Longfellow said that age is no less than truth, just in another dress, and I agree with him too.

4

When we are young, we cry, and when we are old, we weep.

Remember the chapel song we sing:

> *I will weep when you are weeping,*
> *When you laugh, I'll laugh with you,*
> *I will share your joy and sorrow,*
> *Till we've seen this journey through.*

The young cry, for there are many losses, but the young also know how to giggle, for there is far more delight if one will just open his eyes and take a look—your stick collection in the cabinet drawer is an excellent example of what I'm talking about.

Like the beauty of my students' art and their wordy journals and their blooming poems and good music and good food and the moon and the stars and cold water and hot water and oh, it seems there is endless delight here. 'Oh Earth, you are too wonderful for any of us to realize you!' writes my favorite playwright, and I agree with him!

So, keep your young eyes wide open, Teddy, for there is so much here to sing and laugh about. The old folks giggle less perhaps, for we have tasted the deep bitterness of betrayal and stinginess and loss, we know that sting. But when we are old, we also know how to laugh, deep and long and soulful, the kind of laughter that lasts a while, the kind one remembers. Your grandfather and I laugh like that, and your great-grandmother Nanny and I laugh like that when we travel together on long car trips; sometimes I have to wipe my eyes with a cloth while I'm driving because your Nanny makes me laugh so hard. I would bequeath all this laughter to you if I could, but I think you will simply learn it by watching. Pay attention to your mother and father the most, they are extremely good at this.

The old have the young to hold hands with and to climb into tents with and to read books with and to nap with and to giggle with and to stir cookie dough with. It is actually the best of times, or can be. Or should be.

So, my dear Teddy and my long long roster of almost forty years of students, present and past, I want you to know and never forget that as long as I have it to give, I will give my attention to you. My soul is healed by you, just as Mr. Dostoevsky said.

unafraid of

imperfections

> Once you are Real you can't be ugly, except to people who don't understand.
>
> Margery Williams

The beach is hot, even in the morning hours the sand threatens to scorch the children's tender feet as they race to the shade of the bright blue beach umbrellas running parallel to the clear blue water. The surf is big today, waves far stronger than normal, for last night's proud storm with all its fire and bluster and noise stirred up the waters of the Gulf of Mexico, reminding the beach-folk and anyone else paying attention who's actually the boss around these parts. This morning the children want to surf on the large waves left in the wake of the storm. We young mamas slather sunscreen on the many freckled faces and fronts and backs and arms and legs and gather up tubes and Boogie boards and swimmy-rings and goggles and beach chairs and drag the entire lot across the long long bridge to the beach and stake our daily claim on the sand and then head out to jump and jump and jump in the tall, salty waves.

A gift of a day drenched in sunlight and salt.

mornings

Throw us, Aunt Shari, throw us high! the children holler, so I pick up little kids and pitch them over the white swirls of froth to my ready sister-in-law who tosses them right back, again and again, all shrieking in grand laughter with our mouths wide open. One among us—me—all of a sudden feels a little fishy and with minimal searching finds a not-so-small minnow squirming in the bottom half of her swimsuit and when she pulls the wriggling fish out of her swim bottoms and holds it up to show off her catch, the happy group shrieks in laughter even more, loud and long, and the children dive under the water just to pop back up and laugh some more and dive back under.

A gift of a day drenched in sunlight and salt.

Finally tired, we all plop satisfied for a rest under our umbrellas with juicy-drink-boxes and Saltine crackers and plenty more sunscreen and warm sand. Quenched and slathered, the children calm for a few minutes. It is in this quiet that my niece notices my hand for the first time, this little hand of mine that has tossed her in waves for a few summers already and held her tight while her mother changed the diapers of her sister and walked down the beach beside her, she sees me just now, fully for the first time. Her spine straightens, and I watch the questions form in her huge chocolate four-year-old eyes. A grand moment for me, her wide gaze teetering between my eyes and my little hand, her neck straight, posture formal. She senses it might be impolite to ask but her question is simply too powerful, and I know it will certainly cross her lips, for it must. But for now, she stares and wonders.

As I've grown older, I have come to not only embrace but actually enjoy the moment when people first notice my little hand and arm, when they slow down and look and really see for the first time my physicality. This moment of vulnerability is breathtaking for me still, I have not outgrown its startle even after all these years. The beauty of vulnerability outweighs awkwardness every time.

These are important times, perhaps the most important, moments when one's brokenness comes into the light, when error or weakness or disability or crime or sin lies open and vulnerable on the examining table and the Inquisitor shines her bright searchlight on the wound. A person reveals much by how she reacts when she first sees and realizes another's brokenness, *and*, of course, how she views and reacts to her own.

Christ and his disciples came upon a man blind from birth, and his disciples' first question right-out-of-the-gate was, Rabbi, who sinned, this man or his parents, that he was born blind? These men see another man's brokenness and move immediately to assumptions. They demand the facts: tell us *who* sinned, we have the right to know the truth. And while we are at it, also tell us *why*, because we need to know where to place the blame.

Such a simple question; who sinned? This is the question posted on the sign at the trailhead of pride's path, that demanding path without humility or gentleness or the meekness of the Spirit; the world's broad way.

And yet there are those who allow compassion rather than hubris to lead them into the quiet lanes of the merciful. I have met a few, can call a few by name, I've read about a few. Gentle folk who take the time to clean their glasses and try to see more fully, who try to see others through the spotless lenses of grace, men and women who invite meekness to lead them. These precious few folk care less about whose fault it is—the government, the liberals, the conservatives, the police, the school system, the church—and more about the actual person who is broken.

Jesus replied to His disciples, 'Neither this man nor his parents sinned, but this happened so that the works of God might be displayed in him.' I imagine the disciples often leaving dissatisfied with Christ's replies, often confused by the hidden meaning in his parables. What do you mean no one has sinned? the disciples demand to know, thinking they deserve direct answers and sooner rather than later. And while God will respond, His answers are so rarely clean, hardly ever tidy.

And while we're at it, what does it even mean when He says that 'this happened so that the works of God might be displayed in him?'

Folk without grace arrive at the scene with stones in hand. There will always be stones to throw, always those who see the specks in other's eyes while some odd plank is hanging precariously out of their own. Only for those wearing the spectacles of grace is the speck in another's eye almost impossible to see, for the grace-filled are not speck-hunters.

Speck-hunters, can you lay down your stones for one brief hour? Does someone else's brokenness have to be about *you?*

We are looking through the wrong glasses, and the tragedy is we do not know it.

My young niece's brave question finally makes its debut while we rest under the umbrella, her blue juicy-drink spilled down the front of her red-polka-dot-swimsuit, but she, unlike the disciples, is not interested in blaming nor is she demanding answers. She doesn't care who sinned, the humble do not think this way. She simply wants to better understand this odd and wonder-filled life and, in particular, the life of the imperfect aunt she loves. Mustering her courage, she opens her mouth.

When did you get those three fingers? is her wide-eyed query. Her mother looks at me with cautious grin and my wink says,

mornings

No worries, I know how to tell this story.

You know, I got these three fingers and this little arm when I was born, I say, this is the way God made me. Thus begins my lifelong, well-intentioned, rehearsed speech on the beauties of uniqueness, the running narrative of my life. We are all different, I say. Some of us are tall, some short, some dark-skinned, some light-skinned, some with curly hair like me, and some with straight hair like you. An endless listing my niece patiently tolerates as she drinks her juice.

When I finally finish my litany, I ask, Do you have any questions about this, sweet-pea? She does, but only one, an important one.

Will you have three fingers tomorrow, too? she asks.

I smile. I will.

Why?

Pause.

Sometimes this happens so that the works of God might be displayed.

The next morning shines white-hot as our clan stumbles its way to the umbrellas again, beach gear and drinks and children and snacks and sunscreen, enough stuff for six days alone in the backwoods on some reality TV show. My little niece runs to me quick, first thing; she has awakened with a new question dancing on her lips, as well as a new answer. She grabs my little hand fast to take a look.

You still got those three fingers?

I do.

It's OK, Aunt Shari, she begins with a huge grin. her answer polite and prepared, as her mother taught her. It's OK because God loves us all just the same.

From the mouths of babes. And poets. And saints.

Gentleness and kindness toward the brokenness of others is what we must teach and be taught, for this holy kindness is the birthing place of empathy. Without kindness, so much is lost, too much. Without grace, civility and godliness wane and all that's left is intentional cruelty, which, of course, is barbarism.

My niece's mother is a fitting teacher, weaning her daughter on goodness, equipping her not just for today but for always, understanding that a childhood of kindness blooms into an adulthood of grace, and when she is old, she will not depart from the beauty of this ebb and flow of enlightenment. Which, of course, is older than the sea.

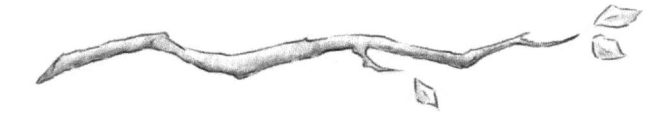

cognizant of

footwear

Who is standing in my shoes, alone?
Bulleg Shah

Consider for a moment the existential weight of one's daily footwear. Have you given any thought to the idea that whether one chooses to wear cowboy boots or flip-flops or sneakers or scuba flippers on a given day might matter, no, might actually change the course of that person's entire life, or at least the timing of things both small and grand, in an ordinary day in that life? I humbly suggest we consider our footwear with care—the fact that Cinderella stood shod in glass slippers seems to bear great weight in her story, for one never knows when a prince might appear.

My daughter is eight months pregnant and sits atop the cold table in the tiny exam room at her doctor's office, trying to remove her boots. She wore tall boots to work that morning, professional and stylish, but it is now the late afternoon, and with the girth of her profoundly round belly and her newly-swelling ankles, she cannot manage to get her own boots off her own feet. Tug, tug, tug, to no avail. These days this new Mama struggles even to reach her own feet, thus the pulling required to remove these now-over-snug boots simply demands more than this new Mama's got left in her.

Sliding from the table, all pride abandoned, New-Mama stands and pokes her head out of the exam-room door to cry for help from the first kind soul she sees, a doctor, though not hers.

I'm so embarrassed, but could you help me get my stuck boots off? she asks the kind doctor in the hallway. Of course, the kind doc laughs and enters the examination room. New-Mama perches once again on the side of the exam-room table, and smiling, raises her leg to the doctor who takes the situation into her confident, medical hands with a grin and begins to pull the boot off. Tug, tug, ugh, ugh. Pulling shoes *off*, the antithesis of a Cinderella story. Tug, tug, ugh, this time a bit harder, but we insist on things when we must. One tall boot finally budges and slides off into the doctor's capable hands, and then the next. But at exactly the same moment the second boot relinquishes its mighty grip, New-Mama's amniotic waters break, at thirty-six weeks, four weeks shy of full incubation. New-Mama's regular doctor arrives on the scene and one quick peek later, two doctors and two nurses and a couple of curious technicians from the general staff who have gathered to wonder (and perhaps giggle) at this highly unusual waters-breaking-at-the-recent-

At exactly the moment the second boot relinquishes its mighty grip, New-Mama's waters break.

-boot-tugging event all agree that it is time for New-Mama to go to the hospital. Right away, do not pass Go.

Did you drive yourself to your exam today? Kind-Doctor asks.

Yes.

Can you drive yourself to the hospital?

Yes. My husband is out of town, do you think I should I call him? New-Mama inquires.

Both doctors, the two nurses, and the variety of technicians now at the doorway all nod aggressively. Yes, they shout in unison, call him right this minute. Do you have someone to call to bring you a bag? Yes. I'll call my mother now.

And so, a new birthing plan is born, such as it is.

But I have nothing to wear, realizes New-Mama, as she and everyone else hovering in the room and at the doorframe suddenly acknowledges that New-Mama's work clothes can no longer be worn out into the world in their current waterlogged condition. A nurse arrives with a hospital gown in hand and a question on her face. New-Mama tries the gown on. What do y'all think? Nope, won't work, the group decides, too risky for driving oneself to the hospital. Another gown arrives for New-Mama and she experiments with the possibilities of a duo-ensemble of one gown for the front and one for the back, but the audience of medical-professional-fashion-critics remains sartorially dissatisfied, shaking their collective heads.

One of the kind doctors flees the scene for a quick second but returns with a pair of her own clean scrubs in hand, blue ones, and *bibbidi-bobbidi-boo!* Cinderella slides into someone else's scrubs, thanks her grand collection of obstetric fairy godmothers, and clad in borrowed robes, dashes off to the hospital ball. See you tonight, her kind Doctor waves a blessing.

But wait. What about shoes? New-Mama's tall boots, the villains of the day's theatrics, barely came off her feet, and then with great struggle; there is no way these lanky waders will succumb to being put back on. So how does Cinderella—or anyone else, for that matter—go to the ball if she has no shoes?

That answer is simple—simply barefoot.

When he receives the text, Almost-Dad has nearly arrived at his speaking engagement deep in the rice fields of Arkansas, a full three hours due west of Memphis.

New-Mom: Turn around and come back, my waters just broke.

Almost Dad: Is this a joke?

New-Mom: No joke. I'm on my way to the hospital now.

Come on home, we are having a baby tonight.

With trembly hands, Almost-Dad turns the car around as fast as a car can reasonably be turned—a bona fide *U-ey* right through the grassy median of I-240 West—and slams the gas eastward toward home, filled with fear that he will miss the moment. He doesn't know yet, nor can he really believe, that he will make it in time, for this ball certainly cannot start without him, and the clock has not yet struck the magical birthing hour.

Barefoot and pregnant, New-Mom shuffles her scrubs-clad way out to the parking lot and into her car and drives herself the couple of blocks to the enormity that is the Methodist Hospital parking lot. Searching and searching for a spot, any spot, she finally parks in a far-off lot and trudges her laborious way toward the sliding doors as if this were any other normal day. But this is not any normal day, for in just a few short hours Time's majestic clock will strike and New-Mom's life will begin again, for this is the way great stories are told.

The lady at the hospital check-in desk looks up and sees a scrubby, barefoot-and-pregnant woman shuffling alone through the sliding glass doors. We are expecting you, the check-in lady chuckles at her own pun and then escorts New-Mom to the room where it happens. Cinderella has arrived. The music (and other things) begins to swell.

mornings

The kind Doctor arrives as the evening progresses, now scrubs-clad herself, the dress code for this evening's fête. A giddy chorus of family and friends and nervous Almost-Dad (who made it on time!) has gathered throughout the course of the evening to cheer the barefoot princess on, laughing and singing and texting and photographing and posting and providing all forms of merriment until the good doctor addresses the group with a grin.

The festivities are just about to begin, the kind Doctor reports. Will you all be staying and joining us?

They will not, retort Cinderella and her groom in unison, and the chorus treks its noisy way to the waiting room to do just that.

But not for long. The delivery room clock strikes midnight, and Cinderella's prince arrives.

And she names him Teddy.

acknowledging

storms

There is peace even in the storm.
Van Gogh

It is the first big spring storm after a long, particularly cold winter. Meteorologist Dave Brown predicts its arrival with great accuracy, almost to the hour, as weathermen do these days, which in this case is somewhere around 2:51 in the morning.

I hear the dog before I hear the thunder. Joe hates storms, most dogs do, I hear. Joe's heavy and panicked breathing arrives at my bedside just before the lightning and thunder, he felt it coming. Joe is either polite or fears being sent back to the kitchen, but one way or the other he remains quiet through the noise of the storm outside, no barking, no protest. It is his breathing that gives him away at the edge of the bed, quick and heavy at the same time, out of control, filled with something like dread.

The air is different in this storm. Thick, warm spring air invades the space of the clean, cool winter air and the two fight for position—warm spring air will win this showdown. The electricity of their fighting awakens the earth and breaks the hard cold ground open for filling. The flowers will appreciate it, but the dog does not. In the morning, I expect, the buds on the dogwood trees will be more fully open than they were on yesterday's walk, and the spring grass just a bit greener.

Things are often much better after rain.

Joe just wants it to go away, he doesn't care about the flowers and trees and grass and the thawing earth. All he can see and feel is the intensity of this moment. The lightning is over-bright and hot and shades of silver light up the room and distort the true color of things, waxing the real and stealing her color, overpowering the real with light and sound. Joe feels the floorboards of the house beneath him shiver and he hears the plates rattle hard on the rack and he is sore afraid. He has neither knowledge nor ability to look beyond this moment.

With every heavy thunderclap, I hear him inch even closer. He will not jump up onto the bed, but he will get as close as he can. One needs companions in times like these, so I lay my arm over the edge of the bed to comfort him. Does he hear my breathing like I hear his? Am I panting as hard as he is?

I am not, although I am now fully awake. I get up and patter through the kitchen to the back porch and open the door. Joe follows close. The birds let me know the storm is passing, and cool air gentle-flows into the kitchen and begins its cleansing. Even in the dark I can see that everything is saturated, crepe myrtles and rose bushes, bright yellow daffodils and the green of new grass, all clean, renewed, baptized—pressed down, shaken together, running over. Joe will join them outside shortly, as soon as the sun arrives to warm it all again. And so will I, to breathe fresh air and hear birds sing and watch flowers grow and remember.

I remember that Behold! once there arose a great storm on the Sea of Galilee and the small boat was covered with the mighty waves. The Man lay asleep but his disciples roused him, shouting, for like my dog Joe, they too were sore afraid. And the Master stood up and spoke to the storm, Silence! And the sea became as smooth as glass. And the men marveled.

And today I marvel. The cleansing power of this storm renews, there is hope in it, such promise. The birds shout and the daffodils whisper the same message—Come out! Do not fear! Be strong and courageous.

The storms God allows, He also calms. Today I will be re-baptized in the promise and be grateful. As will Joe.

believing in

angels

*The angels come to visit us, and
we only know them when they are gone.*
George Elliot

Story carves itself into the bone. Some stories smolder volcanic deep, then without warning, reignite memory and burst into flame on a whisper or scent or song. A good story slams the holy trinity of awe terror and wonder into one terrific storm that shudders the senses before knocking the reader to her knees. And the best stories people often don't believe.

Except the storyteller—she knows.

The year is 1991. The slow train from Budapest to Oradea overflows this hot summer night, room only for standing. When we buy our tickets in Hungary, the stationmaster warns us of over-crowding, so satchels flying, we run like folk on fire from the café to the train station in order to board first and vie for seats. Good fortune precedes us, and we find four together in a small compartment, slam our bags down, and drop exhausted onto the hard seats—'we shall not be moved' the evening's mantra. My husband Larry and

I and Larry's brother and his wife are traveling to visit a preacher, the near-martyr Josef Tson in Oradea, Romania. He is to meet our train at 11:00 pm, we spoke with him on the hotel phone.

So much for the best laid plans.

Everyone wants to go to Oradea this evening, it seems, or on to distant Bucharest, tourists and children and crooks and tramps, the innocent and the guilty, each finds his resting-place in the overstuffed train car, standing, crouching, leaning, sweating, all the fresh clean air is squeezed out the dim windows by the weight and stench of overheated and over-crammed bodies, the air dense with earthy, garlicky breath.

We purchased tickets for the direct train, so our expectation of a non-stop 3 ½ hour trip from Hungary to Romania is a reasonable one. But the further east the non-stop train creeps, the more it stops nonetheless. Wanderers jump onboard unseen by the conductor, a large number of cows and the occasional goat or two that rest leisurely on the tracks from time to time slows things down, uniformed men check passports at border crossings—at one point these uniformed men take our passports away from us and walk away for an extended period of time, many long minutes, my most uncomfortable moment yet—and clutches of stowaways loiter between cars. No one is in a hurry. Although, what I find most remarkable is how the stowaways vanish when the train's ticket-checker appears; I've never seen anything quite like it, before or since. Now you see them, now you don't, it's as easy as that. They simply disappear.

With the constant slowing and stopping, what should have been a 3 ½ hour trip turned into a 6 ½ hour one, placing us into Oradea in the darkest hours of the hot summer night. Our train sputters to a rough and noisy stop around 2:30 am. In European train stations, if the train arrives on tracks far removed from the stationhouse, travelers make their passage to the station through underground passageways, tunnels that keep travelers from having to cross an active railway.

Our train arrives on the tracks farthest from the stationhouse.

We gather our luggage—we rookies have brought *far* too much!—and disembark with the rest of the restless troop of over-weary travelers, but it takes a minute to adjust to the night—not only to the slight breath of cool, fresh air that greets us, but the darkness itself, this night without a moon. It is profoundly dark, compounded by a thin fog that blurs sight. Plenty of lighting fixtures, large and small, line the sidewalks and passageways, ornate in design from a time of Romanian opulence long past, but now none of these fixtures produces any light at all, so the distant orbs of the stationhouse appear cloudy and dim in the deepening fog, like scratchy prints on old film.

Nicolae Ceaușescu, Romania's last Communist leader, and his wife Elena were convicted of, among many things, the mass murder of their own people during the Romanian Revolution of 1989. Before his demise, Ceaușescu ordered the export of much of the country's industrial and agricultural production, leading to extreme shortages and drastically lowered living standards. One of the results of these shortages was that people began to steal in order to survive—bread and milk and clothing and paper. And light bulbs.

The tyrannical Ceaușescu duo was ultimately executed by a firing squad, the only violent overthrow of a Communist government to occur during the revolutions, and it was during the Ceaușescu regime that our host, Josef Tson, was imprisoned and nearly murdered for his faith.

Under constant threats of imprisonment and death for his refusal to stop preaching when preaching the Gospel was declared illegal, Tson endured months of interrogation and intimidation by the Romanian authorities. Not unlike the Apostle Paul and his companion Silas during their imprisonments, God provided miraculous protection for Brother Josef during his years in prison and in exile, sparing his life more than once. During a particularly difficult season of threats on his life, Brother Josef famously responded to the cruel authorities with these words, 'Sirs, your supreme weapon is killing. My supreme weapon is dying. My preaching will speak ten times louder after you kill me.' Fearful of the powerful truth of these martyr's words, the Romanian government exiled Tson in 1981, and Josef and his wife Elena moved to the United States to prepare for the re-opening of the Gospel in Romania, which took place in 1990.

We've come to Oradea to meet him, just one year after his return to his homeland, and we arrive late in the night, and into profound darkness.

Dread may be the weightiest of all things.

Blaise Pascal says 'the eternal silence of these infinite spaces fills me with dread.' Undoubtedly, Pascal was speaking of things more metaphysical than the under-passages of the Oradea train station, but his sentiment resounds nonetheless. In such a silence, the four of us shoulder our multitude of bags and descend into the mute blackness toward the station-house, underground. There exists no other choice. Thicker than the spongy, wet fog that lay on our skin is the palpable fear and dread each of us carries. We can touch it, feel it, taste it on the back of our dry tongues. A weak light at the stationhouse-end of the long tunnel offers a tiny reprieve from our dense, collective tension, but the scratchy sound of a just-lit match brings fear right back as a uniformed Romanian soldier suddenly lights his cigarette in one of the tunnel's unseen shadowed nooks beside us. We gasp at the sudden intrusion and gasp again at the assault rifle at his side.

Walk, keep walking toward the one, small, dimly-lit bulb at the end of this tunnel.

Although the citizens of Oradea have not yet stolen all the lights from the train station itself, it seems that most of the citizenry of Oradea are actually *at* the station in the wee hours of the morning. Well, not the women and children, surely they are at home snug in their beds. As are all the nice- and kind-looking men, men who might actually smile a bit. The citizens who congregate at the Oradea station in the middle of the night are a dangerous-looking lot, the stairs and landings outside of the station filled with people loitering smoking murmuring glaring. Heavy men with equally heavy guns. Not a single smile among them.

This is post-revolution Romania. Ceaușescu has been dead less than two years. Brother Josef is at home, surely wondering about the train, wondering where we are. But no one in the whole world knows where we are.

So, this is what fear tastes like.

We are surrounded by fear and fog and hungry hostile men who ebb and flow around us like a midnight wave in the middle of the dark sea.

The four of us stand in a tight ring outside the station, encircling the small mountain of our over-sized luggage. Larry is the first to break the thick silence with a tight whisper, I'm going to go inside and try to exchange some money so that I can use the pay phone to call Brother Josef and let him know we are here, he says. Wish me luck.

Luck. Luck. Luck.

But we need something more powerful than mere luck. Larry hurries inside while the remaining three of us stand in the blackness, our backs to the absurd number of bags, and come to grips with our state of affairs—we are an attraction, a wealthy American side-show. Gravelly-voiced Romanian men with guns gather around us in clumps and begin to inch our way in small but deliberate steps. We have what they have not, dollars and U.S. passports. Don't look at them, keep your eyes down, my brother-in-law whispers and we know he is right, but the men form a circle around us anyway, so quick, so quiet. No one speaks and everyone breaths hard in this dense and sinister quiet. We are surrounded by fear and fog and hungry hostile men who ebb and flow around us like a midnight wave in the middle of the dark sea. A new-kind-of fear, acutely raw and conspicuously dreadful, is upon us, the kind that scratches in, and stays.

You guys need some help? a young man drawls. Now I've always loved a Boston accent but this one is particularly good.

mornings

Like spectators at a tennis match, the tight crowd collectively glances sharply to the left toward the voice, Americans and Romanians alike. Pushing through the thick crowd is a good-looking, brown-skinned, blue-eyed, curly-haired young man sporting a Harvard sweatshirt and an accent to match. What are you doing here at this time of the morning? This is no place for you, the handsome young man says, stating what every single person in this equation knows to be true, without question. Where you guys supposed to be? the young man asks with a confidence unusual. Oh, by the way, my name is Virgil, he adds and extends his hand.

Virgil—Rome's great poet, the pilgrim's guide through hell and purgatory.

Look, we could use some help, my brother-in-law begins, and unaware of Virgil's friendly outstretched hand, he gives a brief recounting of our need: the train ran late and stopped all the time and we have no way to contact our host. But our problem is far bigger than our story and well beyond the obvious. We are in the wrong place, in the middle of the night, surrounded by a growing crowd of desperate angry hungry men. Antagonism hard and strong interrupts our short introductions with Virgil as the crowd surges again, bristling forward in hostility toward the newcomer. These scowling men do not appreciate Virgil's disruption. They do not know him, I think. He is not one of them.

Tell me who you are here to see? Virgil asks us again, unhurried, un-flapped.

We came to visit Josef Tson, my brother-in-law stammers, Romanian men breathing at his shoulder, touching his arm, pushing him slightly from behind.

You are God people, here to see the God man?

Yes, I guess we are.

Give me just a minute, the Harvard sweatshirt says as he turns to face the crowd. Like a long-armed, long-sought beacon of hope from a distant lighthouse that rises up from a gloom, Virgil raises his right arm to its full length, slow but powerful like a rising tide or a coming tsunami wave, and in a loud voice, the commanding sort of voice that moves men to action, Virgil speaks in a language unfamiliar to us. His words move the crowd, the sound of his voice physically pushes the men back in a collective sway like a strong wind against the branches of thin trees, they blow back as one, with angry scowls and narrowed eyes. A cold silence follows Virgil's voice, dense and tense and wet with the weight of authority, and when Virgil speaks again, even louder this time, epiphany strikes me hard and my chest aches with the magnitude of the moment and aches still at the writing of it.

This is a showdown.

An Elijah and the prophets of Baal showdown.

When Elijah came to *his* moment before *his* angry men, his words sounded like this: 'O God, make it known right now that you are God in Israel, that I am your servant, and that I'm doing what I'm doing under your orders.' And the fire of God fell.

A Christ and the Roman authorities' sort of showdown, yet another group of ancient middle-of-the-nighters who came to harm to arrest, to kill, to do whatever they wanted to do and Christ commanded them to 'Let His disciples go' and the violent mob obeyed.

Virgil's words have the same effect on the Romanian men who encircle us. Virgil speaks his unknown words again, shouts them this time and the crowd shifts again and I feel their tight circle crack. Pushed back upon themselves, these poor, desperate, violent men must make a choice—to fuel their rage and their guns and their threatening stares and attack, or to pocket them all with great reluctance for another time, another place. With glares of hatred and breathy, murmured curses, the Romanian men turn away from the Harvard sweatshirt and away from us. When Virgil speaks one last time, the stairs and landings outside of the Oradea train station empty, miraculous and quick like un-ticketed wanderers jumping from a slow-moving train. No earthquake, no lightning or thunder, simply the power of a Word fitly spoken with efficacious authority, the right person at the right time.

An other-worldly hush falls upon the night sky.

The Harvard sweatshirt turns back to us with his boyish grin. Come on, you guys, I'm a cab driver. I'll take you where you need to be. Few words remain as the important ones have already been spoken. Larry comes back from the stationhouse with a report of no success in reaching Brother Josef on the antiquated pay phone. No worries, Virgil replies as he loads our bags into his taxi. Just get in, I got this. Bags in, we leave the station and speed off into the dark Romanian countryside.

My sister-in-law says these incidents are *etched into her*. She remembers feeling very small in the scheme of the world while riding in a taxi through the dark, quiet, foggy Romanian night. We are all completely spent, we rest our heads on the cool backseat of Virgil's cab. No one on earth knows where we are. Only the stars, and they are usually silent.

Virgil drives us to a nice, well-lit hotel in the middle of the city. I think this is where Brother Josef would want you to stay, he says as he unloads our bags and speaks with the concierge, then he calls Josef on the telephone to tell him that all is well, and then he delivers us, luggage and all, safely to our rooms. Dazed, we followed him like little children follow their teachers, like chicks follow their hen, trusting and without questions.

mornings

Larry and his brother, the brothers-no-longer-grim, try to give Virgil money, to pay him for both the ride and his valiant salvation, but Virgil refuses with a firm hand. A tip at least, they plead, for the man who saved us from the dark of night and its terrors. Boston accent still a sweet comfort, Virgil refuses again, No thanks, guys. I won't take your money. This one's on me. See you around. Disregarding the protests of the grateful brothers, Virgil leaves us unceremoniously, and un-tipped.

We trudge numb to our rooms. We sleep.

Romanian breakfasts are hearty. Plates filled with polenta and hard bread with butter and jam and scrambled eggs and cold cuts and fresh vegetables arrive at our breakfast table the next morning, and having not eaten since lunch the day before, we eat it all, the night's ordeal already tucked neatly into our collective memory. When Brother Josef and his lovely wife Elizabeth meet us for breakfast in the hotel's modest lobby, we tell our story with gusto, all pitching in on the telling of it, bread and coffee in hand, each of us eager with the details of the last few hours.

What a story! we exclaim, sipping strong hot coffee. We cannot wait to tell it back home. Tramps on the train, darkness so thick we couldn't see our feet, no light bulbs, surrounded and touched by an angry mob at the station-house, a driver named Virgil showing up out of the blue.

Can you believe that? An English-speaking cabbie who wouldn't even take any money for his efforts? We don't know what we would have done without him! we all jabber the story at the same time. The details all of equal weight to us, we babble loud and long between bites of bread and sausages, paying little attention to the silent countenances of our host and hostess.

Wonder and strange phenomena are not uncommon for Brother Josef. In his bleak prison years, Brother Josef saw extraordinary things, and like Paul and Silas and other martyrs and near-martyrs in the long lineage of suffering, Josef had a heightened sense of both God's presence and his miraculous work in the dark hours. Finally, Brother Josef speaks, with a tremble in his voice. My dear young friends, you do not understand, Josef begins in his quiet sophistication, removing his glasses to wipe his moist eyes. Providence paid a visit last night. The cab drivers in Oradea do *not* speak English, ever, no exceptions. The English language is too great a commodity here for an English-speaker to merely drive a cab. No one here would *ever* refuse money, under any circumstance. We are a poor poor people, so much has been taken from us, we need many things. There is so much stealing here, so much harm. You were all in terrible peril. There are so many robberies and injuries in these difficult days.

This story cannot be, his wife Elizabeth quietly murmurs, also dabbing her eyes. Your story is an impossible one. Josef looks at us with wonder. You were protected last night with power beyond us, safety sent from God, he said. Apart from this, your story is impossible. Quite impossible.

Three days later we board the same train, heading west this go round.

The apostle Paul teaches us to be kind to strangers, for you might be entertaining angels without knowing it. It seems God sent an angel that dark night, a guardian, and not unlike Dante's guardian Virgil who guided him through the netherworld in his infernal dark night, our Virgil stepped unasked, unconsidered out of the misty night fog in his Ivy sweatshirt and saved us in every way from dangers we now can only think or dream.

evenings

in awe of

night watches

> Dwell on the beauty of life. Watch the stars,
> and see yourself running with them.
> Marcus Aurelius

God birthed the universe in the year of our Lord 1968, in Middleton, Tennessee.

The conditions are perfect for such a birthing. The early summer air breathes cool on the bare shoulders of the twelve eight-year-old girl campers of Cabin 4, privileged to be under the care of a kindly counselor named Freckles. I adore Freckles.

It is our turn for night watch, we've waited long. We tromp noisily to the long pier that juts straight out from the muddy shoreline across what seems the entire length of Kamp Kiwani's seventy-acre lake, and we lie down on the old, wooden pier, skinny chests and faces open toward the night sky. By now, night three of the first week of sleep-away camp, my skinny legs are sprinkled with chigger and mosquito bites, red and welty from constant scratching, and I am sleepy by day's end and only slightly homesick.

Freckles' instructions are clear; girls, lie still, keep your eyes open, and for Heaven's sake settle down and stop talking. And then, to our great surprise, Freckles, the all-knowing counselor, lies down beside us on the pier as if, under this darkening night sky, we are equals or something.

The crickets herald the miracle. Like ten thousand John the Baptists, their feverish scratching shouts the coming wonder the best they can to anyone who will listen, even this bevy of fidgety first-time campers. The crickets know what we twelve do not, that Glory itself dwells in the dark night sky, and if we dare to keep our eyes open, we might witness the miracle.

The Kingdom of Heaven is at hand.

We are lucky, girls, Freckles adds as *Amen* to the cricket chorus, there's no moon tonight.

Several of us already know a few stars, puffed up in the foreknowledge we brought with us to the event—two dippers, one big one little, Orion's belt of three. But Freckles chides us as we speak with the confidence of things already known, already seen. Ladies, you cannot possibly see a new thing if your mouth is open and your mind is closed.

And then, the sky grows one shade darker, and hushes. I watch as a dense white band appears on the horizon and spreads its milky way upward, upward, piercing the darkness. I watch as it towers and stretches its million billion stars from the edge of Kiwani Lake to the very peak of the domed universe.

Glory itself dwells in the dark night sky, and if we dare to keep our eyes open, we might witness the miracle.

Bright stars so dense they form into a gauzy, sinewy giant that rises up like smoke before us, the night sky so completely filled, saturated, that the stars themselves begin to fall from the bulging star-tower to the humble earth in constant streaks of white and green.

And suddenly, in fearful awe of the miraculous, I forget sleep and itchy legs, and even home.

Is it heaven? I whisper.

It is, Freckles whispers back.

Decades upon decades have passed since the summer of my eighth year, and yet every evening I still look for the star-tower from my backyard in the middle of town, though it grows harder and harder to see.

In my memory, though, we girls lay silent on that pier all night long, the twelve disciples of Cabin 4 and our wise wise leader, watching the miracle of the spinning earth, together as one body before the glory of the Lord, and we were not afraid.

examining the

systems

> Our little systems have their day,
> They have their day and cease to be,
> They are but broken lights of Thee,
> And thou, O Lord, are more than they.
>
> Alfred, Lord Tennyson

Sometimes on life's serendipitous paths, two fellow travelers meet and sojourn together for a while. Sometimes these sojourners are poets.

Alfred Tennyson meets his best friend Arthur Hallam at Cambridge, young men, members of a semi-secret debating club called 'The Apostles' that convenes every Saturday night to discuss life and the great questions regarding literature and religion and culture, and also to drink coffee and eat anchovy sandwiches. Sometimes the evenings are heavy and the discussions heated, but sometimes Tennyson and Hallam find themselves lying on the ground gasping for breath from their singular sort of gut-bending, insatiable laughter. Two laughing poets, these guys. They travel together, they spend school vacations together at the Tennyson's place in Somersby where Hallam eventually becomes engaged to Tennyson's sister Emily, and ah! these two fine families will now become one. The two young men plan to publish a book of poems together. Some people call folk like these soulmates; so is it with Tennyson and Hallam.

Two laughing Poets…Soulmates.

evenings

Until Hallam dies.

On a trip to Vienna with his father, young Hallam complains of fever and the ague. With no real alarm, a doctor prescribes quinine and bed rest, and within days Hallam is able to take a walk with his father, albeit a short one. Father and son return to their room for young Hallam to rest for a while, and the elder Hallam, not fatigued, takes a longer stroll alone, only to find upon his return his son slumped awkwardly on the sofa, dead. The autopsy confirms a stroke, and Hallam's body is shipped back to England. Arthur Henry Hallum was twenty-two years old.

This is the agonizing and most Victorian letter the Tennyson family receives from Arthur's uncle, concerning his nephew's death —

Clifton. 1 October. 1833

My Dear Sir —

At the desire of a most afflicted family, I write to you because they are unequal from the grief into which they have fallen to do it themselves.

Your friend, Sir, and my much-loved Nephew, Arthur Hallam, is no more — it has pleased God to remove him from this his first scene of Existence, to that better world for which he was Created.

He died at Vienna, on his return from Buda, by Apoplexy, and I believe his Remains come by sea from Trieste.

Mr Hallam arrived this morning in 3 Princes Buildings.

May that Being in whose hands are all the destinies of man — and who has promised to comfort all that mourn — pour the Balm of Consolation on all the families who are bowed down by this unexpected dispensation!

I have just seen Mr Hallam, who begs I will tell you that he will write himself as soon as his Heart will let him. Poor Arthur had a slight attack of Ague — which he had often had — Order'd his fire to be lighted — and talked with as much cheerfulness as usual — He suddenly became insensible, and his spirit departed without pain — The physician endeavour'd to get any Blood from him — and on examination it was the general opinion that he could not have lived long — This was also Dr Hollands opinion — The account I have endeavour'd to give you, is merely what I have been able to gather, but the family of course are in too great distress to enter into details —

I am, dear Sir — your very Obt. Servt.

Henry Elton

Alfred and Emily, brother and sister, stand together to read this grief-stricken letter, then brother catches sister as she faints, and he eases her gently to the floor.

It is our lot to trust foremost in the systems we ourselves have created and come to expect—good health, friendship, economic success, superior scores on the SAT, and the love of a good man. But in the throes of agonizing loss, Tennyson understands that:

Our little systems have their day,
They have their day and cease to be.

Words he will later pen in one of the greatest and definitely the longest of all his poems.

In dedication to best friend Arthur Henry Hallum, Tennyson produces an epic meditation entitled *In Memoriam AHH*. As the poet grieves in body and mind and soul, he writes on the search for hope after loss; he writes this poem off and on for seventeen years. Tennyson's masterpiece speaks of life and death and the search for meaning within the systems of our living, and finally, after many long years, the poet is able to verbalize some of his feelings of love and loss:

I hold it true, whate'er befall;
I feel it when I sorrow most;
'Tis better to have loved and lost
Than never to have loved at all.

Perhaps this line from Uncle Henry Elton's sad letter spurs Tennyson's metaphysical soul as well as his theological one: 'Your friend, Sir, and my much-loved Nephew, Arthur Hallam, is no more—it has pleased God to remove him from this his first scene of Existence, to that better world for which he was Created.'

'This his first scene of Existence.'

This earth, right now, is where we exist, and it seems no

matter how long we mortals wander around this place, no matter how sophisticated our technology or how wise our philosophy or how beautiful our poetry or how stable our systems, we still wonder the same thoughts as those who wandered before us, those who wrote on parchment and carved on cave walls—what are we doing here? And more, if Uncle Henry is right and this is our first scene of Existence, what then is the *second* like?

Grieving, Tennyson pens:

> *I falter where I firmly trod,*
> *And falling with my weight of cares*
> *Upon the great world's altar-stairs*
> *That slope thro' darkness up to God.*

Thus Tennyson contends that after the inky darkness of the world and the constant trek up a steep-sloping staircase, there is God. So do not be afraid.

Oddly enough, death is the one thing all Creation has in common. But why? Because we are foreigners here, on 'this mortal coil,' as Shakespeare's Hamlet puts it:

> *To die, to sleep.*
> *To sleep, perchance to dream—ay, there's the rub,*
> *For in that sleep of death what dreams may come*
> *When we have shuffled off this mortal coil,*
> *Must give us pause.*

evenings

One of literature's greatest thinkers, Hamlet feels there's something more, a 'dream' that comes after we have shuffled around down here for a while on earth's broad stage. What comes after our 'sleep of death' does indeed give us pause.

Always has, always will.

And Israel's King Solomon, long before the others, joins the poetry with musings of his own:

> *Life, lovely while it lasts, is soon over.*
> *Life as we know it, precious and beautiful, ends.*
> *The body is put back in the same ground it came from.*
> *The spirit returns to God, who first breathed it.*

The wisest of the ancient kings of Israel, Solomon pitches his thoughts onto this ever-rumbling existential bandwagon. He knows what he knows, that when our time here is finished, our spirits return to the One who gave us our first breath, our first Breather.

Arthur Hallam died of a cerebral hemorrhage and is buried at St. Andrew's Church in Clevedon, Somerset. I once visited Alfred Tennyson's grave in Westminster Abbey, London, where he is interred after having succumbed to influenza. Mother Teresa is buried at Mother House in Calcutta, having died—most ironically—of heart failure, while Abraham Lincoln rests at Oak Ridge Cemetery, Springfield, Illinois, his cause of death, ballistic trauma. Diana, Princess of Wales, died in a car accident and lies in Althorp, United Kingdom.

My mother's mother, Jewel, is buried in New Hope Cemetery, way back off the road in central Mississippi in a place called Scanlon Community. The old church and cemetery sit in the fork of two red clay roads where tall Loblolly pines stand as regal guards over the graves of all my ancestors on that side of the family. So many of my mother's people died alcohol-related deaths, an ever-failing system. On our last visit just last summer, my mother and I stood before three tidy graves, those of her mother and brother and uncle, and after a brief pause, my mother said simply, Well, there lie three drunks, and she was not wrong.

My father's mother, Zada, rests in Decatur City Cemetery beside her husband Charles.

My parents bought plots at Memorial Park Cemetery in Memphis. My mother found them at a good price on the Internet (Craig's List, I think, but don't hold me to it) and my father lies in one of those plots as we speak. My mother's gravestone is already inscribed beside my father's, without the closing date.

Alas, poor Yorick.

Truth told, we really don't stay around here all that long. Jesus' half-brother James put it this way, some thirty-odd years after his own brother's crucifixion and resurrection, 'For what is your life? It is even a vapor that appeareth for a little time and then vanisheth away.'

evenings

'All that lives must die, passing through nature to eternity,' Hamlet's mother Gertrude quips to her son as Hamlet grieves his father's death while she herself has happily moved on with her life, married, for now, to the newest King.

The country-crooner Jim Reeves stakes this same claim in his song, 'This world is not my home, I'm just a-passin' through.'

And at her grandmother's funeral, my atheist friend's six-year-old daughter asked her where Granny was now. In Heaven, my friend said promptly and then asked me later, Why did I say that? I don't even believe in Heaven, but when it came right down to it, I guess I couldn't look into her sweet face and say that Granny wasn't anywhere at all.

Every generation, every civilization, every congregation establishes its 'little systems,' its ways of being. Throughout history we humans have gathered together in tight little packs to build cities, to invent and reinvent the wheel, to write and rewrite our creeds, to create art, and sadly, to figure out new ways to alienate and protect ourselves from 'strangers.' Like ancient Pharaohs, we continue to build tall walls with the hands of foreign slaves and then build more walls to imprison those selfsame slaves. Hitler and Stalin and their likes have taught us this, as has their brutal fore-brother Cain.

Oh my, how thoroughly modern this mentality is.

So. How are we doing these days? Here's a popular modern

system, an interesting hobby—invent new ways to hurt each other, practice these skills until they are well-honed, then post the videos online. Barbarism lived in ancient days and has been reborn to live and breed on YouTube, you can take a look for yourself, though I do not recommend it. (Ask an eight-year-old if you can't find the channel.) We are neither more sophisticated nor civilized than we've ever been—beheadings and bombings and people running their cars through crowds of peaceful people in an outdoor market in Virginia—the difference these days is that we brag about it online for the whole world to see. What have we learned from our collective history, and, while we're at it, how much have we changed?

'Our little systems have their day, they have their day and cease to be.'

Empires crumble and systems cease, Ottoman and Babylonia, Persian and Greek, Democrat and Republican—even mighty Rome eventually falls. All that lives must die, passing through nature to eternity. Our little systems are broken and always have been. I've had to stop watching the nightly news for the brokenness of our systems can overwhelm me. Indeed, this world is too much with us. Here, on this mortal coil, we see in a mirror that is dim and blurry, our vision here is skewed and it's hard to know what to do.

How shall we then live?

Tennyson writes:

> *They [the systems] are but broken lights of Thee,*
> *And thou, O Lord, are more than they.*

God is more than our systems, more than our own understandings, more than our logic. Christ's odd, counter-cultural teaching defeats the wisdom of earth and the systems of man through paradox, which human systems cannot touch.

Christ was the most enigmatic of men when He walked around down here on Earth's grand stage. Think how confusing his teaching must have sounded to his friends, that bunch of illiterate fishermen and recovering prostitutes and drunkards and tax-collectors and down-and-outers, how confusing he still sounds to us, we modern sophisticates who have made it to the 21st century and are living to write its stories and trying to make some sense of its songs.

'Whoever finds his life will lose it, and whoever loses his life for my sake will find it.' I don't understand this.

'It is better to give than to receive.' I don't like that.

'The first shall be last and the last shall be first.' No one is ever going to do that.

'Whoever would be great among you must be your servant, and whoever would be first among you must be servant of all.' I will be no man's servant.

And one of the oddest of all, 'If a man strikes you on one

cheek, turn to him the other also.' Are you kidding me?

When I juxtapose Christ's paradoxical words with my modern thought and logic, I find myself in a bath of oil and water.

Who really believes such teaching to the point of altering her daily behavior, anyone? Saints maybe, and a poet or two. Young children, the mentally challenged, perhaps. Sometimes the aged, sometimes the poor. People living non-ironic lives, wearing non-ironic clothing, trying hard to lay pride and ego down, people just simple enough to believe that somehow Christ's commandment to His followers is believable, and actually doable: 'In the same way I loved you, you love one another.' Who does this? A small subset at best, if that.

Nonetheless, Love is the *only* thing that will make a change for good in this world. Only Love. Because even when you crucify it, it just keeps coming back.

Uncle Henry Elton's letter about the death of young Arthur sums it up, for me at least:

'It has pleased God to remove him from this his *first* scene of Existence, to that better world for which he was Created.' Christ promises the better world, the *next* scene in Existence.

'In my Father's house are many mansions. If it were not so, I would have told you,' he said.

Maybe my mansion will be next door to two laughing poets. That's a fine enough thought.

confronting

dread

*I cried unto the Lord with my voice; with my
voice unto the Lord did I make my supplication.*

Psalm 142:1

On the morning of my father's death, a black raven of generous girth caws outside the hospital window, still as an ebony statue perched on the sill of a dark cathedral. I sit alone for many quiet minutes with these two souls, man and bird, one indoor and one out, one silent and the other noisy. Like an ancient priest or prophetess called to disrupt the stony silence of the dying, this raven seems to enjoy her raucous morning song. Surely the raven's message is meant for me, the living, for my silent father lies patient in his bed, his ear ever-listening for the music of another kingdom. Silence and stillness are part and parcel of finishing. With the arrival of hospice—those two jolly souls we dub Happy and Happier, one of whom keeps a stash of hard candy in her pocket—the pulsing and beeping and sighing of hospital machinery ceases. As unskilled as I am in matters of death, I understand what this absence of noise means; but because I had not anticipated this silence, neither had I dreaded it. Thus, am I thoroughly surprised to find the silenced machines a comfort.

The noisiness of sustaining a life, the constant clink and clatter of maintaining a person so ready to fly to the world beyond can only be fully recognized when the machines are wheeled away and in their place impotent IV poles stand erect in the corner of the room, the thin guardians of *this* life, silent, skeletal reminders of the futility and fragility of place—yes, *this* place we all eventually shuffle off of no matter how hard we fight to stay put. Maintenance, of self or others, can be a burden so clamorous that its defeat is felt as relief, and a silence a consummation devoutly to be wished. I had anticipated none of this.

But on the morning of my father's death, the enormous raven breaks this comfortable silence with her fussing and beckoning as if she too had heard the gentle morning nurse say to my mother and me upon our waking, Call your family, today is the day.

Where do you come from, Raven, I ask the bird on the other side of the hard hospital window, and what's with all this noisy caterwauling? I put too little stock in mystery and none in augury, but I do wish this blasted ravening would stop, for on this particular cold morning in January, this bird's song feels like mockery. What do you know of human suffering, you callous bird, and especially the misery of dread?

For the last years of my father's life, a decade in fact, I wandered at the edges of the desert of dread—my father fought Parkinson's disease as hard as he could, as long as he could—and as a result of my wanderings, I have determined that dread—the terrible not-knowing—is one of man's great burdens to bear, heavier by far than Sisyphus' stone for at least Sisyphus knows what tomorrow will bring. From my wanderings, I brought back a journal chock-full of questions for this God of ours, and so, for the few quiet minutes before my family congregates around the bed of the dying—my mother taking a well-earned shower, my brother and his wife on their way—I allow the raven to fly me from the silence of Room 304 on a journey to an ancient location that we descendants of Adam frequent far too often.

The gaping black entrance to the Cave of the Unanswerable.

I arrive at the dark entrance dressed in the signature garments of our homeland, the comfortable robes of my own righteous indignation. Straight-legged and knees locked, I stand before the entrance to the Cave in a grand ceremony-of-self, prepared to fling my fists-full-of-demands at whatever God or gods dwell in this darkness. I must wait my turn, though, for the line of travelers before me is long and their bags equally heavy, for we are all born into the same ancient family of folk who, since the dawn of time, have brought the anguish of the inevitable to the Cave of the Unanswerable.

There are so many of us! In my long waiting, I hear the woes and wailings of the others at the Cave's entrance, and I begin to wonder if my litany of questions and demands have become the sole lyrics to the life-song of my threescore years.

My moment finally arrives—everyone gets a turn—and the silent darkness of the Cave awaits. In the clean rage of a stoic with a dying father, I hoist my indignation high and heave my many stones into the dark mouth of the Cave—my trampled flag of justice and my long long lists of logical questions and disappointments and all my unrealized expectations and my tear-stained journal with all its question marks and bits of my faith with all its fits and starts.

I throw my stones at the feet of the God who sits in this silence.

But on this day there is more, my rage is unfinished, my heaviest question yet unasked. Why Parkinson's? I shout into the deep, and Why dementia? and Why such suffering? and Why do the good die the same deaths as the wicked and sometimes worse and Why don't You do something about this system?

[And why *him*?!]

My hands fist themselves. I am aware these are the wrong questions, I know my unsettled soul has begged but one question of God, but standing before Him I am now ashamed to ask it. But my father's labored breathing and his bluing feet and his newest malady, the inability to swallow, underscore this particular quest to the Cave of the Unanswerable, and I stand now nearly empty-handed having flung all my stones save one, the very one I fear to write (*write it!*), much less speak aloud.

Yet, alone at the edge of this darkness, my truest question tempts and fills me with hubris enough to hurl my fury at the Almighty. I thought when this moment came, I'd scream into the deep like a banshee, but what eeks out instead is a whispered accusation bathed in breath and sweat—

['How dare *you*?!']

I hear my question bounce down the smooth walls of the deep Cave, and I hear the echo of my words return as answer.

Turns out, mine is not a question at all, but mere indictment. 'You are God's critic, but do *you* have the answers?' God asked a sufferer named Job. 'Will you discredit My justice and condemn me just to prove *you* are right?'

Unanswered questions, an oddly comforting inheritance I did not foresee.

Her work now complete, the ominous raven leads me back

to the silence of Room 304. Soon this small room will fill with laughter and story and a sack full of hamburgers for the grieving and tears and agony sprinkled with inexplicable joy, for when a great man departs—with eyes wide and a flicker of a smile on his calm face—even the nurses weep.

No dry eyes when the great ones fall.

The raven takes her silent leave unnoticed, perhaps to croak another passing—until her own day when she flies from this field to the next—but she leaves me with this:

I am not unique with my backpack filled with dread and my unquenchable demand for answers. I am a woman who, like the myriad women and men before me (and after) must bury her dead, a woman who lives to see her father rise from the scabs and ashes of one world to the riches and hope of the next. In relief I lay my robes of human logic down. Too much anger and too many questions wear out the soul before the body, and I am a woman who has heard the echoes of a rich life beyond accusation, beyond dread. A woman who can understand that finishing opens the gate to beginning.

amazed by

seders

> Forgiveness is the restoration of the fundamental relationship by God after man, through turning to Him, is set again in the condition of his creatureliness.
>
> Martin Buber

My first Seder changed things for me.

My Jewish students talk about how Jewish stuff is cool, the High Holy Days they celebrate and the ceremonies. Friends have us over to their house for *Sukkot,* the feast of tabernacles, and we sit under a marvelous tent built in their yard with vivid color and reeds and fancy outdoor lights. The food is fabulous, and I'm jealous of how Yiddish words roll off the tongues of my Jewish friends so naturally, without a trace of smugness. The Jewish people I know seem to have this family and sense of community thing together—better than many Christians I know, but that's just me.

So, I am thrilled when a student invites Larry and me to her home to celebrate the Passover with her family, my answer an immediate *Yes!* Excited, with a side of nerves. This is to be our first Seder, and above all else, I want to make a good impression and do the right thing. I call my friend Leigh for a tutorial on Seder-etiquette and a quick brusher-upper on the history of Israel and Judaism in general. I practice pronouncing *charoset* and *maror* and spend a great amount of time on the Seder Wikipedia page.

I do not want to miss a thing; and more, I don't want to mess anything up.

My place at the table is by my student's grandmother, and the moment Grandmother opens her mouth, I am in love. I am unsure how intentional the seating chart is, whether my sitting beside Grandmother is serendipitous or purposeful, but either way it is one of the great seating arrangements of my life.

You shall tell your children on that day, saying, 'It is because of what the LORD did for me when I came out of Egypt,' Moses says in Exodus. Grandmother retells it all that night, talking me through the entire Seder, bending my ear with instruction—the *Haggada*, the *matza*, the four cups of wine, the hiding of the *afikoman*. I cannot recall a more delightful hostess, before or hence. What a night. Grandmother talks and talks and I listen and listen, and from the first moments, we discover a kinship between us.

After dinner and the Passover songs, just before dessert, Grandmother wanders a bit from the story of the children of Israel to that of her own childhood, a child of Israel who

evenings

finds herself living in a labor camp in her own hometown, making munitions for Nazi Germany. How could she know that the young man that would later become her husband was living at the same time in concentration camps, including Auschwitz —he bears the mark B1516 on his forearm. The Eastern European accent in Grandmother's voice becomes both soft and heavy in the early moments of the telling, her *r*'s rolled, and it takes me a second to realize where she is headed. Once I catch up, she is deep in, reaching back, heading to Germany.

Most of her family died in the camps. She thought her mother died in the camps but found out later that her mother had survived and was living in Israel. They never reconnected, never saw each other again, as her mother died of cancer before she was able to visit in the United States. Her older sister actually saved Grandmother's life by making her look older—older sister cut younger sister's hair and put red lipstick on her—so the Nazis would select her for labor. This same older sister's young baby was killed by a German soldier who threw the baby against a wall early in the war. An infant, a baby.

One sister and one brother survived, and that's how she eventually met her husband, now deceased. Grandmother marches quietly from horror to horror in a steady staccato, a rehearsed cadence, almost singing, dodging emotional landmines and the dark, hidden places, I think. I am not the first with whom she has shared her story.

I have so many questions for Grandmother, hard ones I have neither the right nor the courage to ask. How do you do it, how does one handle such loss, how does anyone survive the horror? And look at you now, so outgoing and resilient, you seem so happy, definitely the life of this party.

How do you carry the weight of such pain and loss? Where is it, what have you done with the weight? Who can understand this? The destruction, the loss of all hope, hate so intentional and well-planned that it is exquisite in its execution, giving raw animal pleasure to the man atop the battlement, the one with the cigarette in his mouth, that calm and cool man with the rifle in his hand, yes, him, that one with the smile, the cavalier one who shoots someone's child before breakfast.

I've seen *Schindler's List*. I've read histories of war, I watch the nightly news and see the videos of young girls kidnapped for sex trading, I see those buildings being bombed in Ukraine (just before the commercials for hemorrhoid cream and a vacation in the Caribbean), and I wonder yet again why things don't seem to change much. 'Life's a corkscrew that can't be straightened, a minus that won't add up,' said King Solomon, another child of Israel in a moment of grand ecclesiastical funk. But now one of the survivors sits beside me and pats my hand kindly as she talks quiet, spunky grin on her lips. She is real.

Where is *your* hate, Grandmother?

Late in the evening, now that we are best friends, I dare. I lean in to her, shoulder to shoulder, heart to heart, and ask, quiet and still amid the clinking and clanking of dishes cleared and dessert brought—How? How did you go on after that? I want to know *how*. She nods and sips her water. Perhaps she thinks of this herself, maybe every single day. Surely I am not the first to ask. This *is* the question.

Here is where the story smudges. At the most important moment, the climax of this tale, accuracy fails me. In my memory and in my retelling, Grandmother leans close and whispers in my ear, breathy language blurred with accent and the recollection of pain and burden but also laced with living and sprinkled with joy. Her head tilts toward me; Grandmother looks me in the eye and says in simple profundity, I learned I must forgive the Nazis, for if I do not, they will continue to steal from me all my life. Then Grandmother turns to sip her water and I can no longer draw a good breath.

Later my student gently corrects my memory on this point; Grandmother says she doesn't actually forgive the Nazis, but rather she has made the choice not to be sad any more.

She did not want to lose any more time being angry or sad and wanted to start enjoying her life. She made the choice and now acts on it every day, living out her decision. Your memory of her not wanting the Nazis to keep 'stealing from her' is perhaps the more poetic version, my student says.

It's easier for me to be poetic about the Holocaust. I suffered no loss, no pain. In fact, it seems I can forget about the concentration camps.

We lived for several fine years in Antwerp, Belgium. Incomparable years, really, some of the best of my life. Good travel and adventure and the best food, Belgian cuisine trumps the French hands down in my book. *Fritjes* with mayonnaise, amazing, *lekker*. And from my bedroom window on the tiny fifth floor of our downtown row home, I can see the lighted dome of the largest and grandest cathedral in Belgium, *Onze Lieve Vrouw*. We walk past this *kathedraal* every day on our walk to school.

Twelve miles southwest of Antwerp, near Mechelin, not really on the tourist map, hate built a prison called Breendonk, a fort-turned-prison camp after Antwerp's surrender to the Nazis. It gained a gruesome reputation not only as a place of torture and harsh conditions, but a place of executions as well, a transit camp for prisoners headed to Auschwitz. About 3500 souls were imprisoned behind those fortified walls, 1733 died before liberation.

evenings

I never visited Breendonk. I knew it was there, open for tours 9:30-6:00 every single day. I drove past its exit as I traveled from here to there. I lived in Antwerp for four years and never really even *thought* of visiting Breendonk. Never considered it for our must-see list of things to do while living in Europe. Visitors came and went in our home, but never once did we visit Breendonk. Every concentration camp has its stories, its ghosts in the walls, mournful songs sung by souls lost—but I never went to Breendonk, I never heard their songs. I never found the time, I was busy, you know how it is. Since I couldn't see it from my bedroom window like *Onze Lieve Vrouw,* I guess I just forgot it was over there.

Who am I? Who does this?

I meet a German woman named Martine in my language class, both of us making halting, absurd attempts to speak Dutch. Level One of any language school is certainly one of the most humbling places on earth, and Martine and I spend our afternoons with jumbo headsets on, biting our lips and stifling schoolgirl giggles, trying to roll our *r*'s and answer properly the important, existential questions at hand: *Zal meneer DeVries neem de trein of het vliegtuig naar Brussel?* (Will Mr. DeVries take the train or plane to Brussels?) After class Martine and I go to lunch to practice our Dutch; we need to broaden our vocabularies and discuss things other than the life dilemmas of Meneer DeVries. Plus we both need a friend.

During those happy years, Martine is a wonderful friend. She was reared in Germany and then married and moved to the States for a while—Mobile, Alabama, of all places, not too far from my Tennessee stomping grounds—so she understands my American-ness more than most of my Belgian friends and answers my myriad questions with kind patience. She knows the good doctors in town and is well-read on European politics, keeping me informed on how the dollar is faring in the European market and where the best cheese shops are. Martine is a wellspring of information and good intent, one of my first real friends in Antwerp. Not to mention my competitor in the Dutch classroom, both of us vying for top ranking and both working almost constantly on besting the other with obscure vocabulary that doesn't appear in the Dutch text book.

One day at lunch I start thinking about Martine's age and realize that her parents would have been living in Germany during WWII. It shocks me for a moment, like finding out a friend has been married twice before or that she had cancer earlier in her life—not a bad thing, just a *big* thing you didn't know or never thought of. I want to ask her questions about her life in Germany but don't know what my questions should be, or could be, what is appropriate to ask and, more importantly, what is off limits. I love Martine and do not want to risk offending her, but I want to know what it was

evenings

like living in Germany during that time. And I also want to know if I could possibly ask these questions in Dutch, as our rule is 'No English Allowed' during the first hour of our time together—only if we get really stuck are we allowed to deviate from that rule, and then just for a word or two to get ourselves back on track.

So, I start fumbling out questions about the Holocaust and Nazi Germany in Level One Dutch over a café au lait in the Antwerp market square, not considering the odd irony that the Nazis bombed and invaded the very square where we are sitting—over 3,000 citizens of Antwerp died within a six-month period of occupation.

What you parent say about Nazi? I bumble in Level One Dutch, and follow with, Do you mother and father ever see Nazi? Then, third time being a charm and all, I realize my real question, which I do my best to ask without offense, You is German lady. What you learn in the your school over World War Number II? Martine has been nodding her head since the first question, and she takes no time and feels no remorse in immediately breaking our 'No English Allowed' rule and sets out to tell me this part of her story in flawless classroom English, a story too important for beginner vocabulary.

There are times when one must use words weightier than Level One.

You are not the first to ask me this, Martine replies, and I do not like my answer. During my time as a schoolgirl, the chapter in the textbook on WWII was short, in my memory it was the shortest chapter in the history text. The bare bones. We were at war, there was a Fuhrer, and Germany lost. That's about it. Most of what I learned about the war, I learned in my own study as an adult. It was hard on everyone. At that point Martine looks me hard in the face and declares in earnest, Not all Germans are Nazis. Then she falls silent. Like Forrest Gump, that's all she had to say about that. We finish our coffees and kiss good-by three times in Antwerp-style. *Tot ziens,* Martine. See you next week.

Back in Memphis, my student's grandmother sits beside me at the Seder table gripping my hand, and we watch together as the little children search for the hidden *afikomen*. Questions shake my usually quiet mind, for a storm is brewing in there, an earthquake actually, and I fear my own unmasking.

What if Grandmother knows? What if she finds out I never took time to visit Breendonk, that I just kept forgetting to go? Did anyone tell her that Klansmen visited a college campus near where I live just a few years ago, and that neo-Nazis seem to be on the rise again? Does she know Iago hates Othello because he is Black and a foreigner and a Moor, and no other reason? What would she say if she knew

evenings

that in Martine's German school the chapter on WWII was only a couple of pages long? Does she know that sometimes hate seems to win and in the length of history, we don't seem to learn our lessons very well? Grandmother pats my hand again and looks into my eyes; I don't have to worry or tell her anything, she understands the facts. She survived and lives to smile and clap her hands at the children and capture my heart completely.

Hamlet is right, 'To be or not to be' really *is* the question, and Grandmother has chosen *to be*. Even after utter and complete loss in the camps, she has chosen happiness and purpose, even risking joy and deep gladness. Tonight, she sips her wine and tells her stories and we all laugh. She has chosen life after death, and I have to tell you, it becomes her. Whether she calls it 'forgiveness' or not, her life of beauty-after-pain-unspeakable is one of the most remarkable acts of living I've ever encountered. Those Nazis did not keep stealing from her all her life. Grandmother wins her war.

My student gives me not only my first Seder, but a handful of years later, she also gives me the gift of my first Jewish wedding. The temple is bedecked in beauty and tradition, the bride and groom radiant standing under the *chuppah*. I smile so much that night my cheeks hurt the next morning. I take unauthorized cell phone pictures during the ceremony—please don't tell the rabbi. At the reception I am seated next to the cantor, and I hope I am a proper dinner conversationalist, but truthfully, I've come tonight to sing and laugh and watch my dear student dance the *horah*. When the dancing starts, I leave Larry with the cantor and bolt from the table to join in, but I quickly realize that I am here this night to witness more than participate. Everyone encircles the bride and her groom as the band turns it up a notch and someone fetches chairs. It is then I see her, Grandmother. I spot her across the floor, just starting to dance. I'd seen her earlier in the reception crowd and had wanted to say *hello,* but she was busy laughing with her children and grandchildren, and I feel quite sure she wouldn't remember me.

That is the beauty of grace—a story properly and honestly told, a tale that marks one forever, a story that changes a person, and the storyteller never even knows. She just tells her story as truthfully as she can, and then God breathes on it and it lives to change lives, like a miracle.

Smiling, waving, singing, clapping as the bride and her groom are lifted in chairs high above the dancing crowd, Grandmother's smile tells her story—a story of joy, real and raw, almost painful to look at in its radiance, yet I cannot take my eyes from her.

And then, if this is not enough, a few men produce yet another chair and Grandmother sits and the men lift her

evenings

heavenward and she waves a white handkerchief in the joy and glory and love of this moment and surely this night she thinks not of survival but of life, most abundant. She is sublime. Grandmother has done her best to set down the pain and horror and grief of *then* so there would be room for the joy of *now*. Forgiveness suits her. Something I want, something to be envied, something to choose. I do not mean to oversimplify, for that is certainly not what forgiveness is; forgiveness is never simple. I have no Nazis to forgive, just regular folk and regular pain. But this I know, this I have seen— Grandmother tried hard to set down her weight, to leave poisonous hate behind her and choose life instead. With a childhood stolen and a camp full of proper reasons to hate, she lives to dance and sing at weddings, to kiss and laugh with grandchildren, to breathe free air. To explore the beauty of life beyond the pain.

Forgiveness. Perhaps we need a better richer fuller word in the English language for this interaction, this volitional act of setting a thing aside and choosing a better path. But while forgiveness may be hard to define, it is easy to see. With no burden to weigh her down, Grandmother's feet are free to dance. Grandmother won her war. And if she can, I can.

I stand for a long time at the edge of the circle and watch her. Not even Nazis could break her. She is free.

In loving memory of Paula Berkensztadt Kelman
January 1, 1927 – June 13, 2015

[not] worshipping

comforts

I measure out my life in coffee spoons.
T.S. Eliot

Sometimes we get stuck, cemented even into difficult patterns, relationships, behaviors that cause us to feel isolated and frustrated. The terrible irony of such stuck-ness is that we don't know what to do to free ourselves so we just stay where we are, we keep doing what we are doing and hope, I suppose, for some sort of cosmic deliverance. Maintain the status quo, keep up appearances, and, by all means, rock no boats. I too often find myself floating down this accidental riverway of seeming ease, ever-amazed at how quickly such floating becomes being.

But if I dare to listen hard, lean out of the comfort of my cozy boat and disturb the delicate balance just a bit, bend my ear to the water and *listen!*, just beneath the waves I hear the dull clanging of my own hollow absurd thinking—I won't change any of my patterns or habits and I'll just hope my circumstances will change for me and maybe this will just go away and get better on its own—and I must ask myself of what kind of ridiculous reasoning am I capable?

If I can be honest, I will wonder: why do I stay drifting like this, do I love my own passivity that much? Have I made such a grand idol of inactivity, of quiet sedation, of my own fears, deep or shallow, that now I no longer have the energy to tear the idol down? And while I am at it, where does it even lead, this crooked little route of reticence I so often choose?

But most importantly, do I dare disturb it?

Autumn comes and each time this season arrives my students and I open our Norton anthologies to T.S. Eliot's poem "The Love Song of J. Alfred Prufrock," they to discover J. Alfred Prufrock for the first time and I to rediscover him. I care deeply and profoundly for dear Prufrock, more every year, but I've come to realize that loving J. Alfred Prufrock is a bit like flirting with anesthesia. For poor Prufrock is a stricken man, fearful and shipwrecked and stranded, etherized from movement, lying helpless and hapless on the universal examination table for all to see. He is a man who lives his life *numb,* or tries to, and the worst part of it is that he knows he's doing it.

One important fact to know about Prufrock is this: he looks good, and he takes seriously the role he plays, that of a middle-aged, middle-to-upper-class man of ease and sophistication. His trappings are correct—tie neatly tied and fashioned with a proper pin, white pants perfectly starched and pressed. I'll wager he carries a cane sometimes, just for the seeming refinement of it, perhaps to impress the ladies. To his great dismay, he's balding, a fact that nearly overwhelms him for he speaks of it far too often [Will you still accept me incomplete, without my hair? 'Shall I part my hair behind?']. So, he practices his comb-over with great hopes pinned to this endeavor.

Like men before him, Prufrock yearns for companionship, for the love of a woman. 'Let us go then, you and I' is his first beckoning line, but we soon realize that he is incapable of making a decisive move of any sort, and (spoiler) he never does. He never pursues a woman or an argument or change of any kind. He closes precisely as he opens, he ends where he begins.

Poor etherized Prufrock.

Prufrock, why? Why don't you move, will you tell us your fear? 'Oh, do not ask, What is it?' he whines in response, spending stanza after stanza discussing everything but the question at hand. So, instead of answering, he wanders in and out of afternoon tea parties (or PTA meetings or doctor's visits or the regular gossip in the carpool lines or—God help us!—on social media) with the smooth ease of privileged familiarity, hands filled with cakes and ices. He meanders through the half-deserted streets of his lonely mind and recognizes the ugly sameness and yellow dirtiness that seems to be settling on everything in the modern era, but refuses to speak about what he witnesses around him.

If it's not that Prufrock is unaware of himself and his surroundings, then what is it? Speak up, man! Why so reserved? What are you hiding? But he does not like my urging, he rebuffs my gentle push. 'Oh, do not ask, 'What is it?' he whimpers yet again. He desires more tea and less talk, a man who prefers his own sedation.

After much protestation and wandering, the procrastinating Prufrock finally finally finally mumbles his angst. Therapists call this a 'doorknob confession.' The client spends fifty minutes of the fifty-five-minute session talking about everything under his particular sun—his sad childhood, his wife, his stupid boss, his greedy kids, his simple bad luck—everything except the real problem the therapist does not yet know. Then, as the client stands to leave the session, the client takes the doorknob in hand and turns and asks over his shoulder, Oh yeah, also, I owe $50,000 in back taxes that my wife doesn't know about. Do you think that might be contributing to my panic attacks?

Perhaps.

This poem, this ironic *love song* is Prufrock's doorknob confessional, a sober tale of a man finally facing the question he has spent his entire life avoiding, 'Do I dare? and Do I dare disturb the universe?' He will duck and dodge the pressure of this question before finally sidling up to his answer, over one hundred poetic lines later, but we know his answer long before his admits it to himself.

No! he will finally declare. He does not dare. It is as simple as that.

Does not dare to do what? The list is long, but the chart toppers sound familiar: he does not dare to challenge the status quo of his comfortable upper-middle-class life, neither does he dare to ask hard questions or pursue a partner. He will not speak of the ills he sees in his culture, he is spiritually lax and physically inert, for it is so very comfortable to remain on the padded furniture on which he sits. Too strong is his attraction to the tea parties with lazy afternoon sunbeams, society women 'talking of Michelangelo,' the arms and eyes of the known, his own clean white trousers.

Perhaps it is Prufrock's co-dependent love affair with *comfort* that makes it impossible for him to move, to dare for something more real, more substantial. The idea that he might be scorned or mocked should some tea-party lady misunderstand his point of conversation and giggle, 'That is not what I meant at all, that's not it at all.' This mocking giggle cripples him and his cowardice wins the day and proceeds to consume his life and he dares do nothing to change his comfortable situation.

Poor Prufrock, dour, disappointed, middle-aged man, finds himself at the crossroads where eventually all stand, his moment to take stock and realize the measure of a life, or at least how *he* measures his own life.

Prufrock aside, how then *do* we measure a life in this crazy, spinning world of ours?

Money earned, houses owned, thick stock portfolios, power and status, pretty children, smart, fit spouse. Friends, real or virtual. Measurable satisfaction in a world made to order, filled to the brim with measuring tape. We understand this and so does Prufrock. After long rambling thoughts of art and clothes and tea parties and why he does not dare to approach a woman, he sighs into the line that reveals his deep understanding of his own plight and admits:

'I have measured out my life in coffee spoons.'

Coffee spoons. What does he mean, exactly how has Prufrock measured his life? What are his measuring sticks, his gauges of success? Prufock's habit is to measure himself by small, insignificant things, little spoonfuls. Nothing grand, nothing risky, nothing dangerous. Rather, tiny teaspoons of sugar and tea bags and well-tied neckties and judgmental eyes and proper conversation and fitting in and *not* rocking any boats and, this is key, hobnobbing with the right people. He looks correct, handsome actually, seated at the sophisticated end of a discussion of Michelangelo. But he knows. He knows that he does not dare to disturb this prickly universe, dare not say the wrong thing to the wrong person and risk rejection or even the slightest hint of disdain lest he be expelled, for misunderstanding and misspeaking is the greatest evil and ridicule the lowest circle of hell.

Do I dare disturb the universe?

At least Prufrock is honest with himself. I wonder if I am as honest with my self-measuring as Prufrock is with his? Do I dare to admit what my measuring sticks are? (Do you?)

In the last lines we find Prufrock still wandering, in his mind's eye, solitary on a beach. Worrying about his age and his bald spot, wondering if the comb-over is still a good idea. He frets that his fine white trousers are getting beach-wet and sandy, 'I shall wear the bottoms of my trousers rolled,' he decides, rolling them up against the inevitable waves that come in a messy (but beautiful) life fully lived, choosing once again, forever and always, the clean path of least resistance. Prufrock has dreamed, he really has, of companionship and a richer, sloshier, more daring life but has chosen instead measured safety, and so his aging is reduced to two primary essences—how he looks and what he's missed.

And it is here we leave him, standing on the beach, clean but alone, talking to himself. 'I have heard the mermaids singing, each to each,' he admits, late in his monologue. 'I do not think that they will sing to me.' The mermaids always sing, poor Prufrock; hope sings eternal, and the opportunities to dare disturb this universe are ever before us. I know you know this, poor man—it is you who dares not answer the call.

practicing

active love

Active love is a harsh and fearful thing
compared with love in dreams.
                    Fyodor Dostoevsky

They call themselves The Way, and my grandfather George spends every Sunday morning of his childhood sitting still and quiet in the over-warm living room of one of the members, a large black Bible perched upon his knee. Coffee stays in the kitchen, cups all rinsed by the time Aunt Iva sings the hymn, or starts it, hers the worst voice George has ever heard, perhaps the worst voice in the whole of God's creation, for surely in its long history 'Amazing Grace' has never sounded quite this dissonant, miraculously both monotone and sharp in the same moment like the grinding of an antique organ warming up. Aunt Iva stamps her black-hosed foot as her thick-soled black shoe marks time on the hard wood slats, and the congregants of The Way begin to hum loud and sway and add their rising voices to a slow-but-steady roof-rattling crescendo. The more faithful the follower, the louder she sings. George never sings unless his father glances his way, and then the boy moves his lips in obligation and sways from the neck up, moving his unrepentant head from side to side; no kid wants to get slapped in church, or after. Aunt Irene preaches the sermon when there is one, but much of the time the members read from their Bibles and testify to what God told them during the week—Let's go around the circle now and each give a testimony of God's work in your life. After the testimonials, Aunt Iva sets her metronome-foot in gear again and the living room sings anew. Services with The Way are mostly an all-Sunday affair.

If prayer alone could drag a person from fire to faith, the fine women and few men of The Way would have hog-tied my grandfather George and dragged his devilish unbelief from its certain demise straight up to the gates of Heaven, for this group of the faithful is undaunted, strong in both body and soul. But since God gave us all a free will—read Genesis for yourself, praise the Lord!—a body must make these decisions on his own, and George has far too much living to do to stay on the narrow path of The Way for much longer. He must sit still and quiet during his churched childhood, for in the 1930s children are seen and not heard, but make no mistake, George's ears are wide open, they hear it all; no drinking, no dancing (except the tiny bit of sway 'Amazing Grace' demands), and absolutely no women. Well, a body can only take so much, and George is a young man with big plans. Plans that include getting out of North Carolina and running out of The Way.

Hope crashes when the stock market does; there is no work to be found in Lexington and George's dream dies a little bit more every day. When young men like my grandfather can't find work, they find trouble instead. A slight hint of madness lies in his eyes; anyone can see it if they take the time to look. Since he was the littlest of boys, Aunt Irene says, he's always been mad at something or somebody. He's got a mean streak in him, and no one claims to know where that came from. As a kid his fury and rage simmers constantly, just beneath his toothy grin, just under the skin. He is caught stealing way more than once—small things in the beginning, after a while a few cars—and he did a couple of short stints in jail, but the moment comes when there are a mere two options remaining for such a boy in the early 1930s—reform school or the military.

Truth be told, my grandfather George never understood contentment, in fact he scorned the idea. Maybe the army'll beat that anger out of him, the good folk of The Way say as they pray over him at his last prayer meeting. The time comes for every prodigal to leave home, this is how that story goes.

In mid-September 1933, my grandfather George joins the army, where he learns to drink.

George finds no contentment in the Army either. The months and years are flat and endless, moving from this post to the next, someone higher up than you always screaming orders, the loneliness of feeling forgotten; he hated it all from the very first day. But what else could he do, where else could he go? 'You'll never make nothing of yourself' was the sad anthem of his boyhood and, in spite of escaping the backwardness of rural North Carolina and the narrow path of The Way, in spite of some tiny successes in his military career, George is not able to silence this song's tune. He doesn't realize that this dissonant melody has become the background music of his life, this ebbing of hope pulsing its steady chorus throughout his days. How can one know there are other songs, when he has never heard them?

The songs of our childhood stay forever and hum deep in our bones.

Hopelessness is a slow-growing cancer, hiding itself in our sinews, lying quiet in the dark places until its time comes. You often can't see it on people's faces, for hopelessness hides deftly behind strained smiles and dull eyes. Left untreated, hopelessness grows rampant within a person, sending its tiny tendrils into the crevices of his life, filling his cracks and crannies with a hard sadness that resists softening.

George needs a change, this fact he knows, but he's never known quite how to accomplish it, for his hopelessness has become his companion, riding alongside him in his army Jeep like a silent twin brother. More and more he feels himself nearing the precipice of despair, fearing the inevitable tipping over but not knowing how to get himself off the side of such a steep cliff. So, he does nothing, changes nothing about himself or his surroundings. Like far too many of the men who came before him, his daddy and granddaddy and so many of the men of The Way and the sad eons of human history, George simply keeps doing what he's always done, with no change, giving no thought to the remarkable idiocy of this plan.

What a remarkable human trait, this tendency to choose stasis and remain unchanged even in the muck and mire of misery. Is it lack of courage that keeps a person fixed? Or could it be laziness? Or simply a scarcity of options? The persistent message of George's childhood is clear—You'll never make anything of yourself—this his only gospel. So, he chose one of the only two options he had, the military, and here he sits. He can never go home again; they don't understand him and they don't want him. Thus, Life's slow clock ticks its steady beat and with every passing day George grows more agitated and erratic, more fidgety, and more mad.

George drinks most of his nights away, especially his Fridays. Payday comes and cash burns a hot hole in the pocket of George's fatigues; the paycheck heads straight to the bar. The drink is George's best buddy, his favorite companion in the long, hot Army nights and in its months and years. 'Booze can be counted on, it's there when you need it and it never tells your secrets, never talks back like women do,' is George's claim. Every prodigal believes that a man is never lonely if he has a boozy bosom friend at his side. Over his Army years, my grandfather becomes adept at many things, masterful at a few; he is a pretty good sergeant, a decent shot, and a consistent poker player. But he is an outstanding drinker, a fantastic liar, and everybody's best friend at the bar. At the officer's club, his pockets are deep and he has far-and-away the funniest dirty jokes. George knows how to keep the crowd laughing, that's for sure.

He is also profoundly adept at slapping people around.

My grandfather George and my grandmother Jewel marry in 1939. At nineteen Jewel is tall and leggy and everyone says she looks just like Barbara Stanwyck—long, thin, aquiline nose, auburn hair swooped back in soft curls, fine penciled eyebrows, gentle hazel eyes. As a little girl, I thought my Mamaw Jewel was the most beautiful person in the entire world as she stood at the gas stove in her tiny Meridian home cooking chicken and hand-rolled dumplings. Like those fabulous actresses of old, her elegance transcends time, and I can still see her gliding effortlessly down the hall and around her boxy den in the full-length royal blue kimono she bought when they all lived in occupied Japan after the war, the gold silken threads a little dingy now, the sash a bit torn, but a soft reminder of who she was during the reconstruction of Hiroshima.

evenings

Even more than Barbara Stanwyck, my Mamaw Jewel looks exactly like Meryl Streep with those high cheekbones and magnificent smile lines. My mother and I cannot watch a Meryl Streep movie without Kleenex in our purses, and when *August: Osage County* came to the movie theater, I texted my mother the minute the closing credits began and said, 'Do NOT come to see this movie. If you want to watch it, we'll rent it and watch from home with bath towels for our tears. This one is way too close to home.'

The only woman more beautiful than Mamaw Jewel was her daughter Pat, my mother, who looked just like her in her youth. They were goddesses in my young eyes. Lord Byron describes a woman like these two:

> *She walks in beauty, like the night*
> *Of cloudless climes and starry skies;*
> *And all that's best of dark and bright*
> *Meet in her aspect and her eyes –*

These are my women. But my grandfather did not see either of them with the same eyes I did. There are many terrible stories.

At thirteen-years-old, my mother—then called Patsy—hears a ruckus in the bathroom of their apartment, her coming-up years filled with more ruckuses than can be named.

Scuffle scuffle, she hears, followed by hysterical, high-pitched screams, blood-curdling and violent. *Thump thump thump* is the consistent bass coming from the tiny bathroom at the end of the dark hallway of their base apartment, and while she runs to see what this could possibly be, Patsy already knows in her bones that her father has had too much to drink and the monster is released. She rounds the corner to the bathroom to see George with Jewel's head in his hot hands, pounding it hard *hard* onto the faucet of the bathtub in a blind rage, all Jewel's beautiful auburn hair flying haphazard like wind-blown Tibetan prayer flags, no words, just low screams and moans and the heinous constant thump of the head-banging bass like a wretched recurring low note in the symphony that portends the inevitable ending of a tragic opera. Stop Stop STOP! young Patsy screams and remarkably the drunk stops, abrupt, and drops Jewel hard one last time onto the cracking tiles of the cracker box bathroom floor. George pushes Patsy out of his way and stumbles blindly toward his car keys and the door, driving off in a dramatic puff of black smoke and noise. Patsy bandages her mother and puts her to bed. No word from father for several, quiet days.

Then there's the one about the poker table.

George and his poker pals are over at the house on a Friday afternoon, the drinking starts early on Fridays. The tottering old kitchen table sways under the heavy elbows of these hard

evenings

drinkers and beer cans litter the floor around the trashcan just inside the kitchen door—the men shoot beer cans like basketballs at the trashcan but they always seem to miss, leaving splashes of beer to soak into the peeling paint of the kitchen and pool up in tiny puddles on Jewel's linoleum floor. Jewel gathers up the cans and throws them away and mops up all the spills as quietly as she can, but the men still yell at Jewel, they all dare abuse her with their demands, Woman, bring us more beer! Why don't you make yourself useful and cook us up something decent to eat? Jewel does what she can to keep the men fed and watered but with drunks it is never enough. She behaves herself and stays quiet in order to keep George's temper at bay, holding off the inevitable as long as possible. Submission is her only plan, and her hands busy themselves stirring red beans and rice simmering on her gas stove, hoping hopelessly that filling the men's bellies will keep them from drinking so much.

It is into this home Patsy strolls every day after school, a young woman with good grades and plenty of friends, destined to be a majorette in just a few years, a beautiful, innocent young girl who wants only what all young children want, for her parents to be happy. And kind. But to her detriment, Patsy is mature for her age, both experientially and biologically. There's my Patsy-girl, George begins the minute my mother crosses the dark threshold of her home that Friday afternoon. Ain't she something? Bring us some more beer, Patsy, your mama's so damn slow. Head down, Patsy passes quick by the poker table and makes a beeline to the small refrigerator to fetch a draught that might quiet the dragon.

What is it about virgins sent to appease monsters? So ancient and primeval, the oldest of stories that through the millennia hasn't changed all that much. This maiden brings the draught to the dilapidated kitchen table, delivers it as she must to the altar over which this dragon resides and then tries to scurry away, but she's not fast enough. The dragon grabs her hard, as dragons do, and pulls her close, breath hot and eyes bright. Their eyes lock for a moment, the innocent and the licentious, and the maiden trembles and her innocent shivers add to the excitement of the moment, and just like that, a maiden once again stands vulnerable before a monster.

The other dragons purr in blurry anticipation.

Lookey here at my girl, turnin' into some kind of woman, growin' up right here before my very eyes, the dragon slurs his speech and before she can think of twisting away, the dragon grabs Patsy's blouse and lifts it up hard, exposing her white bandeau bra to the gawking crowd of poker players. And before anyone can comment or stop him, my dragon-grandfather reaches up and snatches Patsy's strapless bra down to show off the budding young breasts of the virgin standing before them. Let's have a look at them new boobies,

evenings

the villain laughs, and the virgin hears the other dragons purr and laugh as she breaks her father's grasp with a hard slap and dashes away to her room. The rough beast just laughs and slaps his buddies hard on the back. My grandmother Jewel stands wordless in the doorframe of the wilted, hopeless kitchen, wringing her hands.

The virgin gets away, this time.

Where are the heroes? There exist moments in time from which there is no return, moments when a person wakes up the next morning to find herself dead, moments when a person finally doubts her own omniscience and knows in her soul, perhaps for the first time, that she too is a fallen and failed creature. No one can foresee such moments. The seers know, but they never tell.

My grandmother Jewel should have left George years before she did, and I've often wondered why she didn't. She died before I was old enough to ask her these sorts of questions, but my mother remembers and tells of George's constant ridicule and belittling of Jewel; she, this tower of beauty and elegance and intelligence, and he, this angry man with the menacing face, an ordinary drunk, small. Why did she not leave him? Perhaps because a divorced woman in the early 1950s was a doomed state, no systems in places for child care, no reasonable work, no options, no way even to purchase a house or car or rent an apartment without a husband's signature—a divorcee was dubbed a 'Grass Widow' by the society at large.

Or perhaps George told Jewel one too many times how stupid and incompetent she was and how she could never make it without him to take care of her and how kaput her life would be without him. My grandmother seemed to have ears to hear nothing else, she had no other-speakers in her life to tell her a better story, no other words to balance her husband's sarcasm and vitriol with love and respect. No grace-speakers to offer hope and help. So, the scales tipped and she just kept believing the heaviest voice.

Alas, it's a hard enough story to tell, hard even to imagine, so much harder to have lived.

Years pass, like years do. George and Jewel finally divorce and George moves to Mobile—no child support, no alimony, he just up and goes, leaving behind him a grand wake of condemnation and condescension and verbal abuse, a little something to remember him by. George chooses the coward's path, the broad road too oft traveled.

And then one day close to my mother's graduation from high school, seemingly out of the blue, George returns in the gift of a '54 Ford Fairlane—a two-toned red-and-white hardtop convertible he buys as a graduation gift for his daughter. No one sees this coming, not one soul.

evenings

George has the car delivered to the house; unheard of, completely out of character for such a man. Patsy is getting married later that summer, and she and Charlie could use a good, reliable car, but they never dreamed of a *new* car. George always seems to have a pocketful of quick money—he can be lucky at the poker table—but George's money has always been George's money, it has never been for anyone but himself, until now. This wayward father buys his daughter a good gift, an optimistic one.

Perhaps tides actually can change.

Patsy is so proud of this car, its sleek shiny red shimmers bright in the spring sun. Since her parents' divorce, she and her mother and brother have worked so hard and have so little to show for it; to still be this poor after so much effort actually flabbergasts. Patsy works at the florist shop every afternoon after school and has since she was thirteen, and Jewel works as a desk clerk at the Nelva Motel and then as the hostess in a little local dive called The Restaurant where she starts meeting men—but that's another story for another day.

Children of alcoholics all share the same hope, I think, the hope that *this time* it will be different, maybe this time her father will not prove himself as cruel as she remembers him to be. A gift like this car, a gift of this size is new and unexpected, unheard of; so, for this first time since she can remember, my mother senses the prospect that things may be turning a bit, maybe her luck is changing, quite unique in the life of this poor Mississippi girl.

She slides cautiously behind the wheel of her brand-new car for the first drive and senses the presence of a promising traveler beside her in the passenger seat. What is this, she wonders, an attempt at atonement? Hope can bloom in such thinking. Perhaps her prodigal father is turning. Some prodigals *do* turn toward home, as the story goes. Miracles *do* happen, sometimes. It's rare, but that's what makes them miracles, I suppose.

In the last days of the spring semester, Patsy and a couple of her majorette girlfriends head to the student parking lot after school. These are good days, full of firsts, days where Patsy is behind the wheel, the hostess, the girl with a car who takes her friends to the drugstore after school for a Coca-Cola and a few quick minutes before heading to work. She giggles, to feel like a normal teenager is a wonderful new sensation for her, to finally feel a little bit of control in what has been roller coaster ride in her hell-of-a-childhood. For the first time in her life, she feels the gentle breath of freedom, something heretofore unforeseen.

Patsy sees the tow truck first.

The laughing girls are heading arm-in-arm to the parking lot when Patsy slows to the scene unfolding before her, the

evenings

other girls just seconds behind her. In front of her beautiful Ford Fairlane looms an enormous gray truck hitching its garish metal hook and chain to the shiny red bumper of her brand-new car, her symbol of freedom, the emblem on which she has pinned so much hope, too much. Something's wrong, she thinks, this can't be right.

Her girlfriends pause, stop dead in their tracks really, straight-backed, to wait for their friend in the wings of this drama as Patsy must now re-enter a stage on which she had allowed herself to believe the curtain was closing. She approaches the truck slowly, her throat suddenly sore and tongue thick, knowing it is her turn to speak the lines, but oh, how she longs not to have to. Some words taste bitterer than others and lines of a great tragedy are not easy to deliver. In a tragedy, things always fall apart.

Say your line, Patsy, whispers the prompter from the wings.

Sir, can I help you? I think you've made a mistake, are the words Patsy coughs out, surprised at their sharpness as they tear her tongue, as they fall hard on the unfeeling, hard asphalt of this stage floor.

You Patsy Stewart? This your car? the tow-truck-man asks without looking up from his task.

I am and it is, my mother pants just before she panics, for suddenly out of a far-away orchestra pit, remote and covered, she hears once again that odd head-banging bass rising up from some ancient abyss, so unexpected, the recurring music of haunted childhoods. She suddenly feels her shirt being lifted up again for boozy old men to gape at now and dream of later. Odd how exhausted feelings that should be dead-tired and buried-low return to us with the keen speed of new sharpness—they flood with the fervor of a repressed dam, wave over tumbling wave knocks us to our knees, feelings we thought were gone forever return without warning on the lyric of gentle song or the aroma of passing perfume or a hard word remembered, and we stumble. We fall. Patsy falters just a bit at the weight of this swelling tide and takes a quick moment to wipe her tears and assuage the flood, damming it back for now. But make no mistake, the day of the flood will come, it will return. Every dog has its day.

For now, the show must go on.

We got to take this car in, missy, the tow-truck-man delivers his line, finally looking up from his labor. This ain't been paid for, he adds. Who bought you this here car, your daddy? Well, whoever bought this never made one payment on it, never paid one thin dime. We got to take this one with us, darling. So sorry about that. You need a ride home?

Alas, Patsy's one gift from her father is repossessed. A gift unbought is no gift at all, a real gift comes at a price. What she thought was her father's attempt at atonement was simply

evenings

a magician's illusion. Here today, gone tomorrow.

There are no words for hurt like this. These are the silent times, any attempt to attach words to such a moment only insults.

George eventually remarries and settles in Mobile with his new wife. Jewel goes from job to job and man to man before finally settling down once again in Meridian and living out her days in a tiny rental home. Patsy's little brother Mike joins a hippie commune in Colorado and no one hears from him for years and years. Patsy, now Pat, marries Charlie and they move to Memphis where she births two beautiful children and joins the bridge club, the PTA, and the church.

My mother wants nothing more to do with her father, ever. This is her prerogative, for he has more than earned her hate. He stole her childhood and filled the hole in her heart with pain and fear and shame, but she will not allow him to steal her adulthood as well. She makes her way without him, she does what strong people do, squares her shoulders and lives her life. Two earned degrees later, Pat joins the ranks of those in the helping professions—she is both a trained nurse and a trained counselor, digging into her own pain in order to help others with theirs. So many who have crossed her threshold have found hope seated gently on her hearth.

My mother doesn't speak to her father for decades. His new wife sends occasional updates on his health and sends the kids a dollar for their birthdays, but these correspondences are sporadic, and Pat rarely initiates them herself; she prefers the silence. George grows old and his health fails him. A lifestyle of that much drinking and smoking and carousing does not portend length of days, I'm told; add selfishness and a grand ego to the cocktail and it's like drinking poison from ancient, ruined chalices.

And the silent years tick away. Some pain is so deep it takes a lifetime to sort through. So as the ancient tribal drums beat the years away, Pat lives her life without a father. The silence is easier than the possibility, no, the surety of reopening old wounds never accounted for, never acknowledged. George has never said he's sorry and never will, of this Pat is sure. No atonement here, just too much water under too many bridges. Only silent, loveless years.

It's easy to create silent years. Simply let the pen sit still on the desk and do not touch the telephone.

We have only one life, so soon it shall pass. George's wife calls my mother with the news. George is dying, she says, he's in hospice after a terrible stroke, almost dead. If you want to see him before he goes, you better come now.

My mother's drive to Mobile is quiet, and quick.

As the years pass, terror and its aftermath can loom large in the mind, but if you can wait a while and then take a fresh look into the face of your childhood fears, you may find such fears have a way of diminishing. The terrible triplets of anxiety and fear and dread change us, no doubt; they hide deep in our sinews and alter us at our core. Surely anxiety twists its ugly way into our DNA and dread oozes into our bloodstream. But if we get the chance to take another look after many years and see the terror after it has diminished, this experience can change us as well. After a bit of time, if we find a way to look at the monster, we might see there's nothing left but the bones of the thing—like that horror movie that terrified me as a kid, when I see it again years later on late-night cable, it's ridiculous, that weird-eyed doll with the knife in its clutch that rose up from under my bed and tormented my childhood dreams is now ludicrous and sappy and so so small. The chain-saw man in the barn looks fake and frankly no scarier than one's own husband with a chainsaw in the tree tops on a too-tall ladder.

Despite 21st century messaging, anxiety and fear and dread are not guaranteed the victory over human thought and motion. We are not predestined to be the slaves of these terrible taskmasters. We human beings still have strength and the courage to choose our own paths in this world—history and literature support me here, I think. And in her own metaphysical musings of the last years, my mother has been thinking about forgiveness, yes, even for the perpetrator who should have been protector.

'Forgive us our trespasses, as we forgive those who trespass against us.' Forgiveness, a lovely thought but who can bear it, and more, who can do it? My mother knows what it feels like to be trespassed against, we all do. We all have aches deep and hurts wide that require attention, for to be trespassed against means someone intrudes upon us and litters our path with pain.

Someone meddles where she doesn't belong, someone comes and leaves his mark and scar tissue develops, tissue that is calloused and tough and dense. Scars do not simply disappear with time, and nothing really removes scar tissue, especially the profound scars of the heart—except forgiveness, a message my mother has come to believe over her many years working with hurting people.

And now after all this time, the phone rings and the day to test this theory has a time and a place. Tomorrow, in Mobile, Alabama.

George's room in the ICU is small and white. My mother takes her place beside the bed. Her father's breaths are quiet, these are his last days, his last moments, and his room is filled with the muted silence of expectation. George is very old now, and surprisingly small. His figure is slight under the bright whiteness of the crisp hospital sheets. My mother opens her mouth to speak words rehearsed in the quiet sanctuaries of her memory, words she has practiced by herself in solo conversations behind steering wheels and in front of mirrors for longer than she can remember; and yet when the time for speaking finally arrives, no one is adequately prepared. She looks at her father, sees the gray skin of his dying face, sees the blue veins in his closed lids, and the gravity of the moment overwhelms her, her weighty burden overtakes her desire, and she faints cold and falls hard onto the hospital floor.

She wakes to discover two gentle nurses have placed her on a gurney beside her father, a cold rag lies on her forehead. Estranged and weakened by both time and fate, father and daughter now lie side-by-side in twin hospital beds on clean white sheets, parallel, like an equal sign. Both prone before God and the throne of grace. My mother leans up on one elbow and glances at the adjacent bed, looks her dying father in the eye and speaks. I came to tell you that I'm sorry for everything that happened between us, she says. It's taken me a very long time, but I want to tell you that I am sorry for my part. I'm sorry I haven't spoken to you in all these years, and I'm sorry I wouldn't let you come to my wedding, and I'm sorry I haven't let you see my children much. But most of all, I'm sorry I've hated you. My mother's words are quick and reticent.

What an odd irony. Words that take years to sort out and arrange in proper order are spoken with the quickness of a single breath, delivered on a sigh. Said and done. My grandfather lies still among the white sheets and the grace-filled words of his daughter. His moment has come, one of his last. He moves his lips and murmurs his words low, barely audible, with his eyes on the ceiling, never looking her way.

You got nothing to ask forgiveness for, he says and he should have stopped right there, but he could not; he could never stop himself. But anyhow, my grandfather continues, you always made everything so much bigger than it was, you always did love the drama of it all, you know you did. Then silence, and George closes his eyes. No kind word, no thanks, nothing lovely or resplendent to balance the grace offered. George asks no forgiveness in return and admits no wrongdoing, but rather he tosses the blame back on his daughter before he turns his head away from her, away from the light.

It is finished.

A wounded daughter offers forgiveness, finds the strength to extend grace and love to a prodigal father, and the words go unacknowledged with a simple turning of a head. And so, she turns and leaves her father's hospital room and drives back to Memphis. What else is there to do?

evenings

My mother drove down to Mobile lugging with her the heavy luggage of her life: hard-packed bitterness and trauma and rehearsed forgiveness-speeches and years of silence and a stolen childhood and deep sadness. But when she looks into her father's face with forgiveness on her lips and the moment fells her with the amazing weight of grace and she lies prostrate on the floor and faces her own choice of whether to set down her burden or not, my mother opens her hands and releases the bitter stone of expectation. She looks her abuser in the eye and says, I forgive you, yes, even you. That's how strong grace is, stronger than the chains of hate from which my mother breaks free.

Yes, there is an answer to the hate in this world—the better path of grace.

Some people, like my grandfather, refuse to open their hands to grace, we all know this. They clench and turn away, preferring excuses and fists to open palms and mercy. Some folk turn away from the offer of grace and demand justice instead, most do, I think. But my mother didn't. She understood that while she has no control over justice, she has full control over her volitional actions of grace.

My mother chose to try to walk the cobbled path away from rocky ledges of bitterness, a path that becomes a little easier with each step forward. One step at a time, as the saying goes.

No, her father did not 'deserve' her forgiveness, he did not deserve her love, of course he didn't, but who does? There is none righteous, no, not one, says the Book. But my mother chose to open her hands and embrace grace open-palmed, like a child at her first communion, and in this action of love and humility, God broke the curse of her life and set my mother free. She drives back to Memphis to live a good life, a better life cleansed and freed from hate.

[not] being

ophelia

Alas, poor Ophelia.
William Shakespeare

Each September I open the dog-eared, smudgy pages of my worn copy of *Hamlet* to teach this old story anew to a new batch of budding girl-scholars, a tragedy of such epic depths that many call this the greatest of all plays and Shakespeare the greatest of all playwrights, the play about which scholars quip 'everyone knows at least six words.' If any of this is true, then we certainly must read this tragedy that has weathered the relentless winds of time and culture. And even so, my young scholars often begin to read the story with the question 'What's the big deal?' on their lips, wondering whether the hype over *Hamlet* is simply that.

If it has been a long time since you've read a tragedy, then I must remind you, sadly, that most of the principal players die in the end; the last scene in *Hamlet* is a bloodbath, dead bodies sprinkle the stage like scattered threads from a ruined tapestry. But far more than poisoned cups and bloody swords, the last scene of *Hamlet* leaves the reader with a deep-felt reminder that the tragic flaws which so easily beset us all—

jealousy and fear and revenge and overthinking and blind submission—often also destroy us.

By the last scene of *Hamlet,* Polonius dies by stabbing, Laertes dies by stabbing, Hamlet dies by stabbing, Queen Gertrude dies by poison, Old Hamlet dies by poison (before the play even begins!) and King Claudius dies by stabbing *and* by poisoning—quite a villain this Claudius, one who seems to deserve his own double-dying.

Yet none of these deaths brings a tear, not from me at least, and neither from my students. At the risk of sounding cold, all of these royals earn their untimely demises in one way or another, their deaths stinging with poetic justice. Even the death of Prince Hamlet, doomed not only with the flaws of overthinking and procrastination but also with the agony of recognizing his flaws but doing nothing about them until it is too late.

No, it is poor Ophelia whose death resounds, her death that stays with me after the pages are once more closed and the weathered book stored away on the wooden shelf for another year. Ophelia's death lingers with my girl-scholars as well; it is her name that re-enters the discussion in the months to follow, her sad story that finds its way into college essays and senior speeches and classroom art projects. It is for Ophelia we weep. Alas, poor Ophelia, she who is found floating in the brook, her arms full of wildflowers, drowned. But why? Now *that* is the question.

In short, there is simply too much Ophelia lacks.

Poor Ophelia lacks support. She has no women in her life. Neither mother nor mother-figure, no female friends, not even a nurse or maid (Juliet at least had a Nurse and a funny one at that). Ophelia has no women with whom to volley her ideas, no mother's ear for her tender adolescent questions asked with shy-eyes-down at the sewing table, no Nurse to tell her of the wiles of men in general—and of her lover Hamlet, in particular, with whom she has exchanged love gifts before the play begins—no laughter and secrets with girlfriends for Ophelia, tucked away in her lonely Danish castle on the hillside. No coming-of-age discussions, save the little advice Ophelia receives from her brother Laertes concerning her dalliance with Lord Hamlet:

> *Then weigh what loss your honor may sustain*
> *If with too credent ear you list his songs*
> *Or lose your heart or your chaste treasure open*
> *To his unmastered importunity.*

Laertes comes the closest to being kind to Ophelia, concerned about her 'chaste treasure' and all, and Laertes' voice is certainly the tenderest in the play. With Laertes—we are introduced to no other childhood companions for Ophelia, save perhaps Hamlet—we see Ophelia muster the moxie she needs to retort tit-for-tat to her brother's sexual advice-giving, we get a tiny peek at the stuff she's actually made of:

But, good my brother,
Do not, as some ungracious pastors do,
Show me the steep and thorny way to heaven,
Whilst, like a puffed and reckless libertine,
Himself the primrose path of dalliance treads
And recks not his own rede.

In other words, practice what you preach, dude. But after the royal funeral he returned to Denmark to attend, Laertes' plan is to bolt back to college in France as fast as he can, leaving Ophelia once again alone.

And since she has neither support nor companionship after her brother's departure, what Ophelia exhibited in confident sass with Laertes, she lacks in both knowledge and station with everyone else. Ophelia is surrounded only by men, a fact that in no way necessitates disaster in-and-of itself, but the instruction she receives and the self-loathing she learns from *these particular men* does. There is no one to explain to her the ways of love and life, no one gentle with her, no, not one. Everyone makes demands of her, everyone pushes and manipulates her. Her father Polonius is still waving his good-byes to the college-bound Laertes, riding high on horseback toward France, when he grabs his daughter's arm with his free hand and settles immediately into shaming her regarding her relationship with Hamlet. With constant self-serving advice, Polonius pontificates on Hamlet's attentions by questioning *not* Hamlet's honor, but her own:

Tis told me he [Hamlet] hath very oft of late
Given private time to you, and you yourself
Have of your audience been most free and bounteous.

And when brave Ophelia even dares speak for herself to her father of her love, Hamlet,

He hath, my lord, of late made many tenders
Of his affection to me,

Polonius drives her promptly back to her place of shame, concerned, of course, with the grand god of self and his own good name:

Tender yourself more dearly
Or… you'll tender me *a fool [emphasis mine].*

Poor Ophelia asks no questions; it appears no one has given her permission or power to do so. She is lectured by father, her brother, and her boyfriend Hamlet, but she is never asked a question nor does she dare ask one. The men in the play tell her what to think and what to say, and when she attempts to tell her father Polonius of Hamlet's love for her and that Hamlet has tenderly almost-mentioned marriage, 'the holy vows of heaven,' to her, her father taunts her, humiliates her, tells her she is acting like a whore, and demands she stop seeing Hamlet for the damage she is causing to *his own* reputation.

Taken aback, Ophelia musters only a slight, I shall obey, my lord, and with that, the matter is forever closed.

Where are all the women? The absence of women in this drama seems purposeful for the tragedy that is the girl Ophelia, for when Ophelia is abused and most needs companionship, she retreats to her only space, her solitary closet. No friends has she, no older women, no humor or wisdom passed down through story at the washing tub, neither maid nor nurse to tend her physical and emotional wounds. No mother. Just the lonely Ophelia in her closet, bereft of brother and lover, sewing her only company.

The irony of the plague of loneliness in a world populated with nearly eight billion people is wasted on no one—or perhaps everyone.

Dear girl-scholars, even if you are called of God to become a contemplative monk or nun—which is ever a viable option—please do not try to go through this life alone, it does not work out all that well. You need people, you need other women. Seek them out if they are not seeking you out, you must be courageous and do this.

Make amends with your mother, we need our mothers.

evenings

And if such amends are impossible or your mother is no longer in the picture, find another mother-figure, another woman of age that loves you and cares for you. These women exist and are worth every minute of the hunt; try searching the church, the library, the bookstore, your alma mater, a therapist's office, the gym, your mother's sane friends, and keep your eyes open as you go, for they may indeed be searching for you.

And in those times when you are feeling strong and supported, it is then you must remember to seek someone out who is in the midst of her weakest moment. This is our task, our calling. We know what to do, and we understand what comes when we do not act on behalf of ourselves and others, so now we must do it.

Now is always the right time.

For it is not that our Ophelia lacks thought or voice, but rather agency. From the outset of the play, her own father Polonius allies with the King in using Ophelia to try to sniff out Hamlet's perceived madness, a fact that the equally complicit Queen Gertrude knows and does nothing to stop. Ophelia is a girl-puppet in a royal masque much larger than herself, and no one is listening to her, and with no knowledge or encouragement or opportunity or listeners, how can one strengthen a muscle she does not realize she has?

Quiet, blind, verbal obedience is not the recipe for successful womanhood. Poor Ophelia.

And then Prince Hamlet, the man she loves and with whom she has probably been the most honest, betrays her. Wild with grief and too busy chasing ghosts and not-avenging his father's death, Hamlet takes to toying with Ophelia verbally, his favorite pastime. No one (save a gravedigger) can beat Hamlet in battles of verbal wits, least of all Ophelia—she has neither training nor ammunition for such warfare. She is equipped only to cower and take it as he berates her and tries to weasel out of her secret information concerning one of his enemies, her own father.

Hamlet is not truthful with Ophelia, and neither is he kind. 'Get thee to a nunnery' he thrice demands, the insinuation of the phrase doubly painful for its ambiguity, for either Hamlet is instructing Ophelia to save herself against the cruelty of men in the safe arms of the nunnery, or he, this man of words, is devolving into slut-shaming and name-calling—a practice already perfected by Ophelia's not-so-subtle but at least poetic father—and blaming *her,* in common prose, for *his* madness—all the while admitting in the very next breath to his own arrant knavery and that she should believe no one.

If 'I shall obey, my lord' is Ophelia's sole resting place, it serves her not and instead leaves her bereft of hope.

evenings

With a tide of raw cruelty roaring in his wake, Hamlet departs the stage and leaves Ophelia behind, and she finds herself standing alone for her only real speech of the play, the epiphany of comprehending her own wretched position: in love with a man who loves her not, she has heard and believed his sweet vows which now prove themselves untrue, and she sees his once noble mind now overthrown by madness. She is the epitome of woe—

> *And I, of ladies most deject and wretched…*
> *Oh, woe is me*
> *T'have seen what I have seen, see what I see!*

For you see, Ophelia does have a voice, but what is a voice with no audience?

Our poor Ophelia also lacks strength. No one has displayed for her true strength, no, only the deathly rewards of control and power. She is alone, befriended solely by dominance and the verbal abuse that leads to fragility and quiet servitude. The only woman who could stand up for her, doesn't. Gertrude, Hamlet's mother, who sees Ophelia, notices her distress, but is in such a guilty state herself—her affair led to her husband's death—that she has only the bandwidth to worry about saving her own skin, which she ironically cannot do, for the man with whom she betrayed her husband will soon betray her with a poisoned cup. And so it goes. Betrayers betray.

There is no innocence here.

Thus, our pretty Ophelia fades like the clutches of wildflowers in her arms, for the flowers have all withered before her eyes and our Ophelia simply disappears out of sight, quiet and demur and pretty and well-dressed. And with that sad little smile of hers, poor Ophelia heads to the brook, mumbling to herself snippets of old tunes, and quietly goes mad.

Just before she takes her own life.

We hear Ophelia, right? We see her, do we not? She still walks everywhere among us, and we are her audience.

evenings

Girl-scholars, we have encouraged you to find and listen to your voice, to know yourself, to love yourself and others. Do not forget this teaching. Ask your questions well, with dignity and a healthy sprinkle of humility. Demand only when you must but then go forth in courage. Surround yourself with people you respect and trust, people who listen to you and to whom you listen; do not worry if these numbers are few, as they surely will be. Cherish the few trustworthy voices and tolerate the rest but do not listen to unkind, cruel voices; separate yourself from those with great speed and intention.

A young alumna once asked me, 'What do I do when I am overwhelmed and the world is too much with me?'

Seek out the suffering, take care of the poor. Help all who will be helped, and then you must leave the rest, it's all anyone can do. I learned this the hard way, and it took me far too many years.

'Who are the strong women among us, and where?' you ask. Strong women stand up for themselves and fight for others, strong women ask for help and call on other strong women when they fall down, both humble and proud in the selfsame moment. Strong women are mothers, helpers, friends, sisters, activists. Strong women have names like Rosa Parks and Malala Yousafzai and Joan of Arc and Maya Angelou and Dolly Parton; they also have names like Polly and Whitney and Kat and Ashley and Ansley and Abigail and Rainey and Sofia. The strong women are you, and the time is always now. Spiritual work seeks and saves that which is lost. It is time to seek and save Ophelia; she does not 'just get better.' She needs our help.

My own mother has lived her life doing this very thing for women, young and old, and she does it still from her new digs in the retirement community, for she understands that loving Ophelia knows no restraints of time or age, location or situation, and the immediacy of finding and helping Ophelia is the brave, spiritual work of quiet heroes, and noisy ones, strong women at every station of life, helping each other find their way.

To be or not to be Ophelia? Absolutely not.

It is out of the question.

in praise of

pageantries

> I will honor Christmas in my heart,
> and try to keep it all the year.
> Charles Dickens

I am happy to report that the St. Mary's Christmas Pageant hasn't changed all that much in the last 150 years. The pageant began sometime around 1873, but no one knows exactly when. Debuting in the old wooden chapel at St. Mary's Cathedral in Memphis, the Christmas pageant has made her way to all the different locations of St. Mary's Episcopal School over this century and a half, and now resides at the Church of the Holy Communion where the school has chapel every day.

Once a year, a gold-painted, old-fashioned pageant box—a very large open-faced 'box,' recalibrated and reconstructed to fit the new space after the renovation of the nave of the church—houses high school senior girls in framed tableau. Girls clad in multi-colored robes and a variety of head pieces appropriate for shepherds and wise men re-create famous Nativity paintings, while a small collection of angels wear glittery haloes and bless another small collection of Marys who all nestle a common plastic doll, the swaddled baby Jesus, in order to once again show-and-retell the greatest and oldest of all the stories, that of the birth of the baby who changed the history of the world. The pageant is old-fashioned and theatrical, but woe be unto anyone who attempts to alter one single thing about this extravaganza, anyone who dares to change the songs, the lighting, the costumes, the plastic baby—don't even mention it!—for part of the allure of the pageant is this: in a culture that is in constant flux, the pageant stays exactly the same year after year.

Do not touch the pageant. Be forewarned.

Serious second and third grade white-robed choristers march hand-in-hand up the long church aisle, heads erect and hair brushed shiny, their clean faces shimmer in the vermillion glow of their bright red mantles, their young eyes bright with a thousand flickers of candlelight and excited anticipation as all these children take their place on the chancel and become a part of its rich, long history. These songsters sing the songs their sisters and mothers sang, and *their* sisters and mothers, following in the footsteps of the St. Mary's women before them. Did Sisters Constance and Hughetta and Thecla, names that form the early foundation blocks of our school, teach young girls these songs in *their* precious moments at this institution, just before the Yellow Fever came and so many died? Did they sing these words even then, in the midst of such dire troubles?

Sing hallelujah, brothers, Sing hallelujah, sisters
Worship the Jesus Child and praise the Mother mild
Glory to God on high, the angel hosts above are singing
Listen to the story of the Jesus Child.

I think they must have. It's an old song, and an even older story that we gather to commemorate, and remember.

I stand near two boy-babies this year, fine baby-boys with good, strong names, Davidson and Theodore. The girl-children sing their songs about the Beautiful Mother and her newborn Son—the pageant's oldest song, written specifically for St. Mary's—while both of these new-boys sleep, nestled in the confident arms of their aunts and mothers, alumnae who have returned for the pageant.

Beautiful Mother is bending
Low where her Baby lies.

These boy-babies wake and look and listen wide-eyed to the angel voices and then they rest again, at peace, no crying they make. Bright boys these, boys who will grow into strong men alongside the strong men and women in their lives, boys who will know of troubles—because there are always troubles—but who will know of love even more. Just like Mary's little boy. We will tell them the story, our greatest hope, and they will grow in the joy and likeness of the story. Their parents and grandparents will see to it.

Listen to the story of the Jesus Child.

I look over the heads of the two new-baby-boys to see my good friend Orion standing along the side-aisle of the church, just watching all the pageantry, his long arms by his sides. He stands tall among the freshman faces, young girls who do not know him and will not know him. Orion and I have taught together for many years—he Math, me English—unlikely friends, we. Orion watches the pageant with fresh eyes this time around, for Orion is very sick. The tumors won't stop growing and the doctor says his days are short.

Orion Miller is a great friend. He really was.

He listened to me when a congregation we were members of fell apart and left me sad.

He encouraged me to keep writing when I thought I would never find a publisher.

We attended all the school concerts—Christmas and Spring—with Orion and his precious Nancy, but only after Mexican food at El Mezcal, a requisite.

I watched Orion's classes for him while he went to doctor's visits, back when he was still keeping his cancer quiet.

These days I ask him what it feels like to know your days are short and he says, *Weird.* I ask him if he is afraid and he says he is not. I ask him about Heaven and he says he had a dream about Jesus. All is well.

evenings

Emmanuel, Emmanuel, they call His name Emmanuel.

Orion's eyes look forward with great intensity at this year's pageant, the grin on his lips slight, resigned. His senior math students stand in the antique tableau box, clad as shepherds and kings and angels and Mothers, the way St. Mary's girls have stood in that box for so many years and the way they will stand there for so many more. This pageant and its story transcend time, but not memory.

Memory, what a gift! Could it be the best earthly gift? Memory softens things while intensifying them at the same time, it expands through time and gifts the past with an emotional beauty too grand for the present. A gift richer than gold and frankincense, God gives us memory so that we might have flowers in the cold of December.

As Orion stands pensive, he is remembering, I think. I see him watching the tableau and listening to the beauty of the angel choir, but I can also see he's really watching his Nancy and leaning hard on his memories. Orion's wife Nancy is the pageant's inimitable choral director. From my standpoint beside Orion on the east wall, I watch Nancy as she directs—such energy, this one, like none other, really. She stands erect in her bright red robe, the same red as the children's mantles, strong of arms and voice she is, and her directorial hands fly about the church as she leads her child-choir, her enormous smile fully content in this moment. Perfect articulation, perfect harmonies, and for a few glorious moments the room is saturated with the awesome weight of beauty such that one must weep, for there is nothing left but tears. But this day Nancy appears able to set aside the weight she bears, the heaviness of her husband's illness, and she leads us boldly into worship with her husband's favorite pageant song:

A silent night, a baby's cry, a mother sings a lullaby,
A star is watching from the sky, long time ago, long time ago.

And her beloved watches her from his perch in the side-aisle, knowing what we all know, that this is his last pageant.

The pageant is over and the children recess. Orion strolls to the front of the church where students and alumnae spot him and he is swarmed with admirers young and old. Former students hug him and want him to see their babies. He is *papa* to many children, so many, after years and years at White Station High and St. Mary's, and his many children all adore him.

This year's math seniors gave him the tie he now wears, made from a picture of them all at Derby Day, all of them muddy and sweaty and grinning as wide as their cheeks will allow. Orion sports this tie every time he makes it up to school, which is less and less in these dying days. It seems some girl or another is always giving me a gift or a card to take over to Orion's house—I visit him every week—and they all contain the same simple message, written in neon yellows and pinks and greens and laced in bright red hearts—*I love you, Mr. Miller*—which we all know is not a simple message in the least.

So. The pageant concludes and the girls go back to class. Life goes on, as we all say when there's nothing else to say. Orion finds his Nancy at the front of the church and gives her a gentle kiss and tells her what a fine job she did on this year's pageant. This pageant is different for me, more special, more vibrant, more intense than most. Surely it is because of the dying man standing in the side-aisle and the two boy-babies these alumnae mothers have brought for him to see, and perhaps to bless. May these boys grow up to be strong men like Orion Miller, I pray, and as I watch the old man grin and love the young boys he will not be around to know, I weep at the terrible beauty and awesome glory of this life that encircles us all, every single day, with joy.

Joy to the World, the Lord is come!

Orion and Nancy walk slowly down the aisle toward the door, hand-in-hand, like always. I will remember this pageant-day forever, for to see love given and received is a glorious and perfect gift. Just like the Baby was, and is.

So today we sing *Glory Hallelujah* even in the midst of troubles, for this is our hope. Sing it loud like the second graders who lead us and the senior girls backstage singing in their final pageant and sing it for Davidson and for Theodore and for Nancy. Life goes on.

Sing it for Orion, and remember.

> *Hallelujah, Glory Hallelujah*
> *Our hope forevermore.*

In loving memory of Orion Columbus Miller, Jr.
January 25, 1948 – March 30, 2016

choosing

hope

Hope is a thing with feathers.
Emily Dickinson

On an ancient afternoon, a defeated king walks on his bare exhausted feet across the windy plains of Troy, alone in his anguish. His battle forever lost, his lone last desire before his own death is to retrieve the body of his slaughtered son Hector for proper burial, but the body is in the hands of his foe, the great Greek warrior Achilles who refuses to return his victor's prize. Achilles who chooses instead to deface the fallen Trojan warrior further every day by dragging his body in mockery behind the grandeur of his own victorious chariot. In spite of this humiliation, Old Priam, the decrepit king of fallen Troy, plods onward in his hopeless mission, walking steady in the calm of his complete despair.

A journey of total futility.

Head down, tired bones creaking, the king carries nothing with him, save this—the sliver of hope that flickers in every human heart despite all odds—the hope of mercy, the deepest hope of all. After crossing the weary plains, this king humbles himself and kneels before the slayer of his own son and kisses the very hand that killed his boy, then lays his hoary head onto the lap of the Achilles, this murderer-of-men, to beg for mercy and his son's body. Mercy—even the thought of it sparks a tiny fire of hope in this fallen father's heart, and so King Priam pushes his knees forward into the stubborn sand and humbles himself and begs with the ridiculous hope of mercy from a madman.

The apostle Peter's best friend is arrested and tried in the middle of the night before a mock court that finds him guilty of treason against Rome. The penalty for such treason is crucifixion; the law is the law, and this law will be exacted the very next day. Peter, feisty and bold in the early hours of the evening with his sword drawn, ready to slice off the unexpecting ear of a Roman sentry doing his duty, now grows quiet as the night hours turn toward morning. Thrice he spoke the same words—'I don't know that Man!'—damning words *so* quickly spoken without a thought, those proverbial save-your-own-neck-first words that we common folk say a hundred times over every day, and the memory of this saying sits like dust in Peter's mouth and he cannot drink and he cannot eat and he cannot look but down. The cock crows the arrival of the morning sun on crucifixion day, and the words of Peter's friend, the one who claimed to be the Messiah, the one in whom Peter pinned his hope, float in on the sun's first rays over the quiet sea, whispering the only sentiment Peter can hear—'you will betray Me, three times over, before morning.' And now it is morning and the prophecy is fulfilled. Peter turns away from the night fires.

Perhaps Peter will go to the crucifixion site, for the written story says that those who knew Him would watch from afar. But perhaps Peter simply makes his way to the seaside alone, to a familiar place. His friend is gone and he has betrayed the one he loved most; all is lost, so who cares? So, Peter goes back to the sea, to his fishing nets, for where else do those bereft of hope go, but backward?

The four little boys—four! boys! all stair-stepped about eighteen months apart, oh my!—who live across the street from me jump on our trampoline most days after school, and every day that they jump, they come to my front porch with their father, ring the doorbell, and ask me, Please, Miss Shari, may we jump on your trampoline? I tell their father early on that there is no reason for the boys to ask me every time they want to jump, for the answer is a standing *yes,* but even as I speak, the father shakes his head *no.* No, no, the father says, these boys need to learn to ask politely and then say thank-you. Say thank-you, boys.

Thank you. Thank you. Thank you. Thank you.

This daily goodness goes on for weeks and weeks, all throughout the lovely fall of the school year. My doorbell rings and four little boys in unison ask permission and I say yes and they say thank-you and then I watch them from my kitchen window as they jump higher and higher with each passing day. Sometimes I bring them cookies, but I don't think their father wants them to eat too much sugar before supper, so mostly I just watch them from the window. If I were an artist, I would have drawn or painted them all by now, over and over. I love these boys, and their patient father who is raising them well.

One afternoon after school, the doorbell rings as usual, and my smile leads me to open the front door where this day I find a solitary soul, the father, standing by himself. His shoulders low, an orange UT ball cap pulled down almost covering his eyes, hands deep in his pants pockets. When he looks up, I see his tears. What is it? The oldest has been diagnosed with leukemia, the father's voice breaks. The boy and his mother are at St. Jude now. I'm home to pick up some clothes and let the grandmothers into the house to take care of the younger boys.

evenings

I need to pick up a few things for my boy (pause), a choked cough and then the father can speak no more. We just stand there together and shake our heads at the heartbreak, the uncertainty, the confusion, the lack of logic, and most of all the fear, the grand overwhelming fear of loss.

But St. Jude, he finally says, is right here in our city. The doctor says there's reason to hope, he says there's always reason to hope.

Sometimes, often actually, stories end well.

Priam, the king of fallen Troy, lays his ancient, weary head in Achilles' lap and begs for mercy—all that's left—and the mighty Achilles relents and returns his son Hector's broken body for proper burial, procuring an afterlife for Priam's son among the gods and the fallen. And Priam is grateful, even for his enemy.

The apostle Peter's friend Jesus rises from the dead, who could have ever thought or dreamed or imagined *this* outcome? Peter hears the news and runs to the tomb to see it for himself, but alas, Jesus is not there. But shortly thereafter Jesus appears on the beach where heartbroken Peter has spent a fruitless night fishing, and Jesus cooks Peter and his friends a fish supper over their own fire. 'I will go to make a place for you,' He tells his disciples, 'for don't you know that all must die in order to live? Have I not told you?' Death before life, this is how the story goes.

And the oldest neighbor boy, the one with the biggest smile and the highest jump and the biggest voice and the leukemia diagnosis, he graduated from college last year and is out looking for a job.

It seems when all is lost, when the rough seas of despair and loss rage high and loud, the only respite in the fear-filled lonely night is hope, thrown as a lifeline for the sinking, for hope is often all that's left, a thing with wings. Hope is energy, it pulls and pushes and lifts us from the murky lowlands to higher places, drier hills on which to plant our heavy feet.

Certainly hope is a choice.

We want to know the way things are, and more, we want to know why. So, we ask the stories of great literature and all texts ancient and modern that pass on to us the tales from generations past to show us the way the world is, to chronicle for us the human experience, its foibles and blisses, its pains and prejudices, its cruelties and passions. We tell stories to remind ourselves we are not alone, to acknowledge with gratitude those who have trod before us, and to examine the movement of God and gods and of men and angels. We want to know how other people live this life, across the ocean and across the street, thousands of years ago and yesterday, why we worry and what we talk about as we sit down to our dinners of an evening. Over what do we universally weep and do we share similar joys?

Do we recall what lies at the bottom of Pandora's box of woes? Hope.

The greatest of the bards—Homer, King David, T. S. Eliot, Shakespeare—remind us that there is really only one story, and that this struggle of good and evil must have a stage, a backdrop for its drama, wings where we players can stand to deliberate our next steps and make our choices, and the magnificent playhouse built for this grand drama is the human heart. Amidst all the muck and mire and joys and wonder lies the deep Edenic gift, the great human legacy—choice. The choice to see and embrace the grace and beauty of this odd, paradoxical life, and the hope that one can choose redemption and stand again. Beauty can be birthed from the ash heap—in fact, it most often is—and what remains through all the toil and tribulation is hope, the antidote to despair.

There is always room for another resurrection story.

afternoons

searching for

two skies

> And from the midst of cheerless gloom
> I passed to bright unclouded sky.
>
> Emily Brontë

Two skies exist side-by-side in my view of the Alabama summer beach, fighting, it seems, an ancient battle for who will win the day. Two skies so completely different one wonders how they could exist at the same point in time and within the same panoramic view. Soft shades of hopeful morning light streak across the eastern sky, pinking and bluing the horizon, and grand mountains of orange cumulous clouds pile in an endless stairway toward heaven. I strain my eyes looking up and squinting at the rising sun, for on a morning like this one, hope can be reborn, if one will allow it. And yet with a slight twist of my head from left to right, I see wholly different sky, ominous and dense in hopeless gray.

Oh my, how remarkable that threat and hope dwell in the same moment, both a mere tick of the clock, a quick turn of the head away.

Six enormous gray rain cells line the western horizon, already emptying themselves into the sea, and the three large fishing boats I've been watching all morning have simply disappeared into this mighty dumping. One of the dark cells blankets Mobile to my right and I wonder if the good folk of South Alabama are not standing at their windows, looking out and crying, 'Surely the end is near! The Second Coming is near!' But if I turn my head to the east, I see that this apocalypse is momentary, I can literally see the end in sight.

The cells out in the Gulf are merging with the giant cell over the Alabama flatland to create a massive beast, spreading from Mobile to Destin perhaps, I cannot know, and lightning flashes in glowing streaks across the dark horizon. Loud peals of thunder rumble in anger, and in mere minutes whitecaps form on what were easy, gentle waves.

And yet the storm is still in the distance, it's not yet here. I sit and watch people on the morning beach set up shop for the day, staking their claim on the sand with coolers and chairs and tents as if there were no storm at all. As a huge, gray cloud bank crawls its way down the beachline, a lady in a flowy white shirt arranges her chairs under the two blue tents she just erected, and from my vantage point on the thirteenth floor, this lady does not seem in a hurry. I have to wonder why she is setting up her tents *before* the storm,

afternoons

can she not see it coming? Is she not watching in fear and trembling? Those tents are going to blow all the way to Panama City, I say to myself. What in the world is she thinking, what is going on here?

The gullywasher finally arrives. Heavy rain falls in enormous white drops, far bigger than snowflakes, and the gray sky covers us, erasing the horizon completely. Nothing left but storm. Bowling balls of thunder and electricity. The last few beach-walkers and the crew of young guys who set out the beach chairs and the lady in the white shirt all sprint for cover.

Only gray remains. I sit on this colorless porch surrounded by storm.

This storm takes its time, content to stay put for a while, in no hurry to travel from this beach to the next. The white waves grow larger and hit the shoreline in tall, angry bursts, and Larry and I watch and wonder about the storm's power and how long this all might last.

Surely the end is near, the Second Coming is near.

Finally, after a while, a faint, hazy snippet of light reappears on the distant horizon, and a single light white cloud eases its way into this bluing. Then another. The sky above Mobile Bay clears a bit, and an unusual July breeze blows chill. I look at the woman's tents, still erect. Despite the wind, her preparations hold. This is not the Fury that will destroy the woman's tents, this one not the apocalypse. Not this time, not yet. Uh-oh. I look to my right, and Mobile Bay is once again covered with storm clouds, but now I know something about this particular storm, its dark-clouded bark is far worse than its bite. What you see is not what you get.

This storm will pass, it is passing already.

I've been around, you know, and I understand this is not true of all storms. Hurricanes come and level everything in their paths, and tornados bring chaos and destruction. But not all storms are hurricanes or tornados—indeed, most are not.

Still, things don't seem to change much around these parts. Like the two-faced god Janus who in his day saw both the past and the present at the same time, these two skies declare the inevitability of the coming-and-going nature of storms—it's always been like this, always will be.

Old Daniel faced quite a storm in his day, do you remember his story? 'Worship Nebuchadnezzar or face the mouths of hungry lions' was Daniel's conundrum. That's rough when you believe in only one God and refuse to worship another, when you're a man of too much integrity to perform a sham bowing of knees to protect yourself. But what King Nebuchadnezzar did not know was that Daniel worshipped a God who closes the mouths of lions.

The storm will pass, it is passing already.

And Daniel's buddies Shadrach, Meshach, and Abednego faced the same challenge with the same king. (How is it that kings are so often slow to learn, if they learn at all? Are they *so* filled with their own glory? Perhaps it's best not to believe our own good press.) Shadrach and Company were tossed into a furnace of fire and came out unburned, not even smelling of smoke. Turns out, the same God who tames lions controls fire.

And even so, sometimes hurricanes *do* reach the mainland and destroy—history teaches that from such touch-points heroes and martyrs often spring.

Martin Luther King, Jr. died for his beliefs and for his noble cause in my own hometown.

And Saint Stephen was stoned for his fearless witness and belief.

And Joan of Arc was burned at the stake for rejecting church authority in favor of direct inspiration from God.

And William Tyndale, who translated 90% of the King James Bible into English, was sentenced to death by strangling.

And Sister Constance and her Companions, the Martyrs of Memphis, returned to the city during the Yellow Fever epidemic, unwilling to leave the poor and sick and dying but rather stayed to work when others fled, and they themselves died of the fever.

Lion's mouths are not always stilled and there remains the need of sacrifice, and the good and loving work of God continues through the blood of the martyrs. God allowed His own Son to die. The storm itself is not the end of the story.

This beach storm passes, this one not a devastation. The lady in the flowy white shirt walks back down the boardwalk toward her tents that stand straight and tall like two blue sentinels on the sand—that dark clouds sometimes cover the sun and hide the light is a given on this beach.

The split between our stubborn humanity and the divinity within us is a storm, a constant tension sparked with electricity and fire. My task is to remember that even though the light may be hidden at times, it is never fully extinguished. Look to the horizon and be reminded—not all storms devastate.

People repopulate the beach before the storm passes entirely. The thunder is still rumbling and only one of the two skies has cleared. Poor, dumb, resilient us, willing to get a little wet in pursuit of our spot on the beach, our place in the story. I may saunter down to those tents and meet this woman, my newest fearless hero who prepares her tents nonetheless, even in the shadow of a coming storm. And as she and I stand together to witness dark gray in one sky and cerulean blue in the other, she will remind me that not all storms are hurricanes.

And I will tell her how much I love this old spinning world.

in the midst of

adverse conditions

If you are distressed by anything external, the pain is not due to the thing itself, but to your estimate of it, and this you have the power to revoke at any moment.

Marcus Aurelius

It is a particularly dark afternoon, the kind of quick-stormy day that happens in the springtime in Tennessee, tornado weather. An enormous cold front piles up hard and moves fast across the flat rice fields of Arkansas, straining, heaving its burdensome black cloud formations for long miles, turning day to night in minutes. Outdoor lighting flickers on at noon, this semi-darkness tricks the lights sensors, and dogs cower wide-eyed under beds, they feel the storm coming. My crepe myrtles sway maniacally, limbs and blooms dancing in the frenzy, the wind blowing white and purple summer snow down the street and across the greens of many a well-clipped lawn.

On this most blustery of days, my daughter is coming home from driving school, her newly-earned learner's permit buried deep in her bag, snug in a soft nest of movie ticket stubs and lip glosses, her usually calm mother in the

afternoons

passenger seat. But today is different. It is dark out there and growing darker, straight-line winds predicted to roar in from across the river and those winds don't play.

We are not far from home when the torrent begins, only one more right turn by the Catholic church and then left toward home. Thunder and lightning crack together in unison, no pause between *boom* and *boom*, warning us to hurry on our way. This storm means business, this one packs a punch.

I look on ahead, and I can see what she cannot. Power lines already down, utility workers scurry from their poles, they believe the lightning's message that the time to take cover is *now*. Orange cones line both streets, reducing traffic to single lanes, and the rain falls in sheets. It's dark.

My new driver turns carefully onto our small street and notices the orange cones and the downed lines; her grip tightens, ten-and-two now permanently imprinted on the steering wheel. The daytime darkness is so profound the street lights come on.

You OK? I ask.

I'm fine, is her tense, terse reply, her eyes on the ever-darkening road. This is pretty intense, I offer, pull over if you want to. Plenty of drivers are.

Ever-prepared for imminent disaster, she responds with a direct quote, 'Remember, when adverse conditions arise, rely on your training.'

Mother, I am *fine*, she says in the unmistakable scornful tone of a fifteen-year-old girl-child who possesses that remarkable nothing-can-touch-me-security.

But then another big bolt of lightning flashes and we both jump. That one was close by, I say. With tight hands and eyes riveted to the road, ever-prepared for imminent disaster, my daughter responds with a direct quote from the driving manual on which she took a test just this morning, 'Remember, when adverse conditions arise, rely on your training.'

In school we have drills for such situations—tornado, fire, earthquake, and now crushingly, intruders in the building, for we must know what to do about a person carrying a gun, we must be trained. Drills discipline us to respond well and with as much knowledge as possible when adverse conditions arise—because they *do* arise on this glorious spinning planet of ours, as sure as the sun sets and rises—so that when adrenaline is high and things start falling apart, I've been drilled, I am equipped, I will know what to do.

I've trained for adversity, and now I must rely on my training.

Last week I watched as management in an up-scale restaurant trained some of their junior wait staff, all apparently new to the job. Pushing the hatchlings out of the nest, the trainer stands back as the trainee tells us of the evening's specials, answering our questions and trying ever-so-hard not to glance down at her notes. I like her, she's eager. I hope people are kind to trainees, I say aloud to my table after our server departs for the drinks, but I know not everyone is kind, we've all witnessed it far too often. There are those sorts who thrive on making others squirm a little bit, or a big bit, and that kind of ugliness I find difficult to understand; nonetheless, in the case that such a tyrant be seated at one of their tables, trainees must be indeed be instructed on dealing with the adverse conditions that accompany difficult people lest they stumble when they inevitably find the obnoxiously-difficult sitting at their station, lips pursed and eyes narrowed, looking for prey—you know them, you can spot them a mile away. Everyone can.

Marathon runners train for adverse conditions as well, for what could be more adverse than running 26.2 miles without even a mean dog or a wild boar chasing you? And yet, these runners do, all the time, all over the world. When my husband ran his (first and last) marathon, he trained for months and months, enduring the inevitable aches and pains of life and limb that accompany the disciplined training of a long-distance runner. And on marathon morning, cold and rainy as it was, these runners were undaunted, for they had trained for difficulty.

And don't forget the children. Not long ago, my grandson climbed too high in a tree, far higher than he meant to climb, and when time came to come in for supper, he was a little scared to climb back down. Come on, his mama said, you climbed up, now you must climb down. One foot at a time. After a quick beat my seven-year-old grandson took one step down and then shouted with great confidence, Don't worry, Mama, I don't give up. I have grit *and* distress tolerance (clearly his mother, the trained counselor, has been filling his eager first-grade brain with language for the inevitability of difficult moments).

Adverse conditions come, no one is exempt, poll the world and you will see. And COVID did a number on our tolerance levels that we have yet to measure or correct, if ever we can. It will take a while, we've got much work to do.

Nonetheless, in this writer's opinion, what we *do* in adversity is the key that opens the mysterious door of who we are, this is what defines us, our training ground. How we handle adversity is the peephole to the soul, for this proclaims our training more than anything else.

One of my favorite poets, Gerard Manley Hopkins writes, 'What I *do* is me.' Amen, brother. If I ever get a tattoo, this will be the phrase I commit to ink.

When really pushed, really squeezed during 'adverse conditions' as the driving manual promises, if I dare to pull out my magnifying glass and examine honest and hard, just underneath the surface, I will see who I really am. And if I dare see who I really am in hard times, then-and-only-then can I do something about it. This is a fact, and thus to deny it must be deemed foolish.

considering the

lonely

Thou shalt love thy neighbor as thyself.
Mark 12:31

If you believe the music, it's the happiest time of the year. Cards and candy and family and festivity and tinsel and toys. From the moment the first decorated tree appears in Target—in mid-October, mind you—until the last coin is dropped into a Salvation Army kettle outside of the neighborhood Kroger, Christmas is the season of music and miracles and giving and receiving. But not for everyone, I am reminded on my family's first Christmas far far away from home.

While wonderful, our first Christmas in Europe proves entirely different. For one, there are no boxes of decorations to be brought down from the attic as our things have not yet arrived from the States, no stockings hanging by the chimney with care for these expats, for we are living in a small, furnished apartment with an over-over-used red vinyl couch in the living area and an army cot in our daughter's room, décor certainly not destined for the December issue of *Home Interior*. So as our thirteen years' worth of collected Christmas treasures lay dormant in a shipping container somewhere in

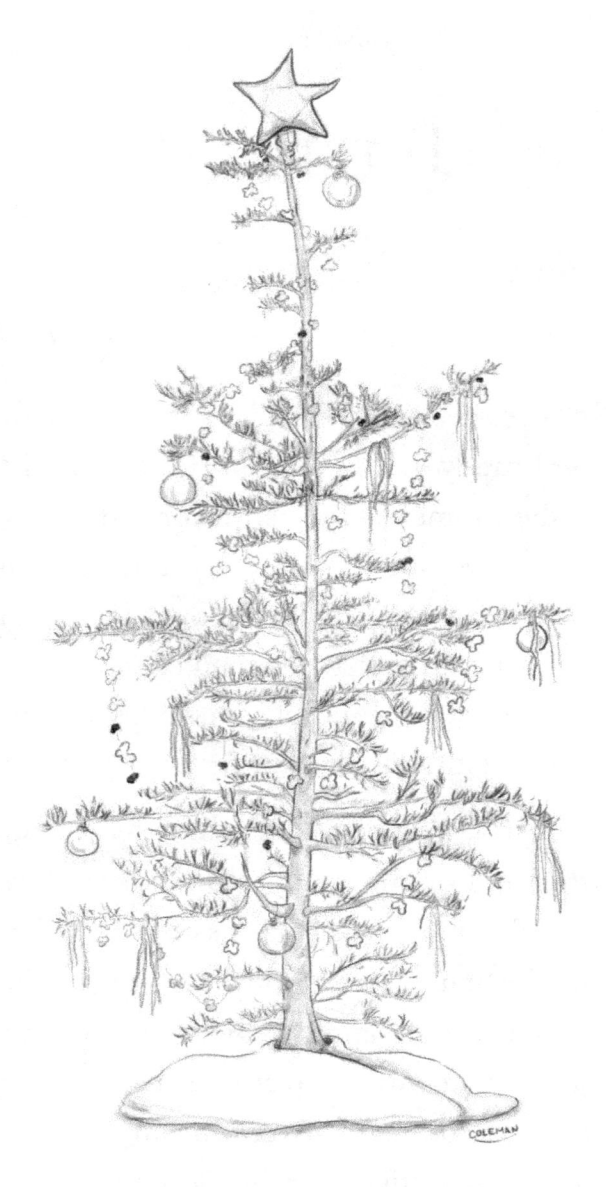

Ribbons and tinsel—strung popcorn and cranberries—topped with a foil star, it filled our tiny new home with the spirit of the season.

afternoons

the Atlantic Ocean, we decide that maybe an old-fashioned Christmas is in order. We buy a small tree from the lot by the park in the *Fruithoflaan,* our street, and adorn the small thing with strung popcorn and cranberries, bedeck it with many-colored ribbons, embellish with tinsel thrown only as high as a seven-year-old can throw the stuff, and top the tree off with an aluminum foil star. Much more like Charlie Brown's tree than anything found in the fine Antwerp store fronts, but for us it was beautiful and it filled our tiny, new home with the spirit of the season.

My seven-year-old daughter goes to work on a nativity scene, creating Mary, Joseph, the baby Jesus, and various farm animals out of construction paper, paste, and glitter (yes, much glitter) which we will tape on the white walls of our cozy kitchenette, and I begin working on the Christmas cards. Christmas cards have been a significant part of Christmas for us, and these were to be our first Christmas cards sent from our new overseas home, so they must be special, unique to our time in Belgium. Maybe I'm a sentimentalist, but I find it all quite remarkable.

I write the cards early that year, as I have much to say regarding our recent move and our gorgeous new city of Antwerp. Rainey and I walk the cards to the post office on the last day of November with great ceremony and send them around the globe, then walk the short block home to drink spiced tea and add a little more glitter to Baby Jesus' manger.

The first week of December comes and goes. I check the mailbox every afternoon, sure that all of my friends back home are as eager to send me Christmas cards as I am to receive them. We receive lovely cards from both sets of our parents, but that's it. Not to worry, it is still early in the month.

The second week of December, no cards. Week three, the same. The two from our parents hang pitifully from the otherwise bare door frame in the living room. I finally tape one of our own extra cards up there so the whole thing would look less pitiful, but this act produces quite the opposite effect.

The fourth week of December we finally receive a card from a language teacher we met in our first language class. Ironically, I had forgotten to send him a card. Still no cards from the States, and it becomes increasingly obvious that we are not going to receive any Christmas cards this year. I could not believe it or understand it. I sent so many cards and quite early in the season, I might add. We had always received so many Christmas cards from friends, former students, colleagues, college acquaintances, and neighbors. But this year, nothing.

The problem, of course, is not the Christmas cards and I know it. The problem is that I am living in another place, far away from the normal hustle and bustle of this wonderfully hectic-and-overly-busy season, and I feel as if everyone has forgotten about me, way over here across the waters. I am lonely. Not lonely for people necessarily, as we have many acquaintances and already a few good friends. I am lonely for familiarity and normalcy, lonely for the laughter of friends and being entirely too busy, lonely for the smells of food in the teacher's workroom of the school where I taught, and for my mother's enormous Christmas trees, lonely for what all my friends are doing now without me. I am lonely because I feel forgotten.

My Christmas without Christmas cards gives me a glimpse of a lonely world in a way that nothing else ever has. Through feeling alone and forgotten, God opens my eyes to other lonely people in the world. For the first time in my life, I can share a little of their pain and understand just a bit of the despair of loneliness. For in the forlorn faces of many around me—the old man in the park on a cold bench, the woman sitting alone in the corner of a café—I see loneliness personified, and the Spirit moves within me and seems to say, Now that you too have tasted the tiniest morsel of the bitter fruit of loneliness, what will you do with this bit of pain that I have graciously allowed you to experience? Will you follow My example and open your life to those around you? Will you look around and notice who sits alone, will you help to melt the cold, empty feel of loneliness with a genuine act of love?

Christmas cards in hand, I accept the challenge. What else am I to do?

I knock gently on the door of the concierge of our apartment building. I notice that you don't have a Christmas tree, I begin. Yeah, she remarks. I don't usually celebrate Christmas, no one to share it with, you know. We have coffee together, and she tells me a bit of her story—her husband died last year and she has no children—and I tell her a bit of mine—this is my first Christmas away from my family in the States. I talk about the message of love that belongs to Christmas and I give her a card, the first one she has received in years. You will come back? she asks as I take my leave. Oh, yes, I'll be back.

I visit my elderly neighbor who lives alone, no family, no visitors. I take her a card, and we share a cup of tea. She shows me pictures in her worn scrapbook and speaks of faded memories of her son who died many years ago. She listens as I talk about the miracle baby born many Christmases ago. She enjoys the message of the Christmas card so much that she keeps it on her kitchen table until February. Would you like to come to my house next week for tea? I ask as I rise to leave. Oh, yes, she says without pause, so very much.

The gentleman at the bank, the lady at the bakery, the bus driver, the man sleeping in the deserted doorway, the mother standing alone at the school, waiting for her child. Lonely faces, grateful for a smile, a word of encouragement, and a Christmas card proclaiming a message of love.

I begin to realize that what I am experiencing is not loneliness at all, but simply a hefty shot of justified self-pity based on Christmas cards and the lack thereof. Please, a little levity, I say to myself. But my eyes are open a bit wider now and my spirit can see some of the empty sad desperate people who may feel as if the world has forgotten about them. And maybe the world has, but God has not. If God wants to set the lonely in families, as he says in Psalms, then how is this to happen? In a moment the answer becomes obvious: through me, through my family. Our families are to be earthly pictures of a greater family, the family of God. How else will the lonely and desperate of the earth ever see God if they do not first experience His love through someone close by, a neighbor, whom we are called to love as ourselves. When I direct my focus from myself to others in an attempt to alleviate their pain, God Himself tenderly eases my own.

There is a happy, predictable ending to this story. Two days after Christmas, our postman François arrives at our door with his hands full of cards, letters, and even a couple of boxes.

You must have a lot of friends, is all he says. We see François every day that week, bringing my long-awaited Christmas cards. The Christmas rush combined with the time it takes letters to go across the ocean simply brought us our Christmas cards a little late. I had not been forgotten after all, just shuffled around a bit in the frenzy that is Christmas.

But I do hope the faint bitter taste of loneliness forever lingers on my tongue, for I am a far better servant neighbor lover helper friend when I do not forget the empty feeling of the forgotten.

finding

homes

> How often have I lain beneath rain
> on a strange roof, thinking of home.
> William Faulkner

I have my doubts when my husband Larry starts hanging out with street people, namely a small clutch of men, six or seven guys who walk and gather and sleep in and around Poplar Avenue in Memphis. These few guys and Larry go to lunch, they sit on shady bus benches and talk through the hot hours of the Memphis summer. Sometimes they go to dinner, often enough that the staff at the local Burger King learns everyone's name and one night late, just before closing, the evening manager gifts the group with a small mountain of hamburgers destined for the trash bin.

As I said, I am uneasy about these new friendships in the beginning and the amount of time Larry spends with these guys, but I can't put my finger on *why*. I begin to wonder if it's possible for me to gather up my apprehension into a tidy bundle in order to look at it and poke at it and examine what my odd unease actually is and from where it comes.

Is it fear I'm feeling? Or judgment? The heavy weight of

preconceived notions, perhaps? Or worse, is this disquietude actually the ugly, biting beast of superiority, that grand surety that I am smarter cleaner nicer harder-working than someone else, especially these street guys who I was sure—without knowing a single one of them yet, not even their names—could find a job and get off the street if they really wanted to.

The confidence of having the upper-hand is an opiate, the surety that one knows everything about everything—and therefore is right about everything—is a drug-habit hard to kick, most addicts die in its clutches, I fear. Such superiority begets itself, and if it remains unchecked will reproduce exponentially and become one's way of thinking and being; eventually such positioning bores into the deepest part of our souls.

Turns out, my own unease is fault enough. Perhaps I need to place myself under the clear eye of a surgeon who, this time around, must operate on herself, a patient in desperate need of an amputation—something about me has got to go. Or maybe I need to set aside the tinted glasses I wear that prove (to myself) I'm better than the average bear. One way or the other, I stand in the wings of this particular drama and keep my mouth shut and watch in wonder as the curtain opens and the complicated plot begins to unfold.

It doesn't take long before I start to recognize people on the street as we drive up and down Poplar; the small group of men who live under the bridge at Poplar and I-240—Steve with the crushed face, Fred who rides his bicycle all day long, all over town. We stop at red lights and before the light changes have quick-shouting conversations through open windows that sound something like this: Pete, how are you and Roger doing? You guys need anything? Naw, we're good for now, but thanks. Y'all hungry? A little. Why don't you guys meet me at Burger King in an hour and we'll get some supper. OK, we'll be there, thanks.

Larry's Nissan begins to look like a storage closet—coats, shirts, boots, towels, blankets, backpacks—now I know where many of the Memphis folk without homes store their stuff. Or at least some of them, the folk who stay in and around the environs of Poplar Avenue. I start finding other people's things all over my house—Jimmy's antibiotics in my refrigerator, right beside the milk. Luke's frayed tee-shirts in my dryer. Sleeping bags and space heaters and small mountains of sports socks and blankets form their own congregation in the corner of our garage. As winter approaches, coats miraculously appear from nowhere like loaves and fishes.

Larry loves picking up people on Poplar and taking them where they need to be. The Russian writer Fyodor Dostoevsky claims that 'every man needs a place to go,' and of course, he's right, there's always somewhere we need to be.

Even those dealing with homelessness, especially them. To the courthouse to work on getting an ID. To the post office to receive packages from relatives. To the drugstore to pick up medicine. To the Salvation Army to get new shoes. To church.

Larry's new friends start coming to our church, and I have to admit not everyone is enamored with the idea. To be fair, helping those who have little-to-nothing is more trying when somebody steals your wallet out of your purse right in the middle of church. Those without homes are not always the most gracious lot, as those with homes might wish.

William with the waist-length dreadlocks meanders in and out of the church service constantly and not without noise; though frankly he wanders around no more than the regular attenders in search of another cup of coffee or the bathroom, but somehow William's movement seems more egregious to some. Frank sometimes shouts out at inappropriate times, blessings and curses right in the middle of the sermon, and he lacks all discretion in his colorful language choices. A large cardboard sign graces the entire front part of Sally's walker and reads HOMELESS, HELP! Not to mention, Sally has a wonderfully unique fashion sense that includes enormous hats and yards and yards of toile and plenty of cleavage. Pete snores through every service with the vigor and volume of a sleep apnea patient. Nobody can sit still in

afternoons

their seats, everyone fidgets and sleeps and stands up when the rest of the congregation sits down. And somebody smells bad, *really* bad. Some of the mothers hold their children a bit closer when these street-folk drift by to visit the table with coffee and doughnuts or to roam in and out of the front doors. Back and forth and forth and back, a restless lot, these guys—restless, but not dangerous.

But still.

When you are friends with a wide variety of individuals, there are plenty of funny stories. Larry takes his friends to Burger King most every Sunday after church. What he quickly finds out, though, is that when you take five or six street people to lunch each week, it is much easier on everyone—the purchaser of the food, the restaurant staff, the other patrons, various and sundry onlookers—if everyone would simply order the same thing. It's faster and otherwise the entire process can become quite complicated, for it turns out that, just like everyone else, those without homes have distinct culinary preferences:

I'll have pickles, but no ketchup.

I said extra mustard.

I told you last week, no onions.

What do you mean you don't carry Pepsi products?

Turns out, special orders actually *do* upset us, so Larry decides that the best way to handle all the special culinary needs is to order everyone the same thing—the #1. Wherever this fine crew dines, Larry generally orders the #1 for everyone. At Burger King, though, Jamey doesn't like the #1, he prefers the #3, and he is adamant on this point. Like the rest of us, Jamey is an expert at grumbling, a trait inherited from our forefathers at the dawn of time. Thus begins the big Sunday lunch Burger King Battle Royale. Rain or shine, Larry pulls into the Burger King parking lot after church, and he and Jamey bolt from the car and sprint toward the restaurant doors in an all-out hamburger footrace, trying to be the first to the counter to shout the order. Larry wins most of the time—we'll take six #1's!—and the reason for the easy win is not complicated; Larry is simply younger and spryer. Believe it or not, life on the street can take its toll, and Jamey has been out there for a long while.

afternoons

On one such Sunday Larry sprints to the counter and once again beats Jamey to the draw. Disgruntled as ever, Jamey shuffles his feet around and complains to all within hearing range that he *never* gets what *he* wants, a #3! and How hard is that? and Why is Pastor Larry so mean? and Who needs this crap, anyway? and I ain't coming back no more. An amused lady stands in the line behind this motley crew, just watching, and after his ordering, the lady leans over to Larry and remarks, tongue only slightly in cheek, Well, turns out beggars *can* be choosers, can't they?

Hmmm. It would be funnier if it weren't so true. For aren't we all, some of the time (most of the time?), a raggedy crew of fault-finding beggars just searching for the comforts of home?

Another time in another city, our daughter Rainey and her husband Coleton take their youth kids to downtown Chicago to pass out food to the street folk there. Coleton has sacks full of food for the kids to give out—peanut butter and jelly sandwiches and packages of cheese-and-crackers and granola bars and trail mix, really good stuff. One of the youth kids is a little shy, having never served people on the street before, so Coleton goes with him to approach a man who has just awakened from his sleeping near the doorway of large bank.

Excuse me, sir, the young boy begins, I have some food here that I'd like to give you, just to help you out a bit.

Whatcha got in there? the man asks, his voice rough with sleep, and life.

Well, hmmm… the boy stammers, crackers and trail mix and sandwiches and…

You got any cereal in that bag? I like Reese's Puffs.

The kid stands quiet for a moment. Um, no, sir, the kid mumbles. He had not expected this.

No Reese's Puffs? Then never mind, I don't want any of that other crap. And in a grand scene of finality, the man rolls over onto his sleeping bag, turns his back on this nervous youth kid with his sack full of food, and dozes back to sleep.

Am I like that? Am I a hungry person who says I need food, who prays for God's provision, who begs God to help and to remember me in my need, but when his provision comes, I roll over from my resting place, albeit often an uncomfortable spot, take a quick look around at what's offered and say, You know what, never mind. This is not what I wanted, this is not what I asked for. I'll take the #3 or nothing at all, thank you very much. No Reese's Puffs? OK, well, if that's the best you've got, then no thanks.

Is this how my prayers sound, if I dare listen to myself? God, I need a bigger house. God, please change my husband wife mother father kids boss neighbor friend. God, I will forgive her, but only if she goes first. God, we need more money, we simply must have more money, show me the money! Demanding prayers from choosy beggars. I seem to recall there was but one leper who returned to Jesus to give thanks for his healing, and his faith and gratitude made him whole.

Pete was the first person Larry encountered when he started knowing the people of the street. From the outset, Pete starts riding around with Larry, going from place to place, making a church visit or picking up food for some of the widows in another community or dropping off clothes at the refugee center. Riding and talking and listening and eating and just being together. The stuff of, the makings of a friendship.

[And the King shall answer and say unto them, 'Verily I say unto you, inasmuch as ye have done it unto one of the least of these my brethren, ye have done it unto Me.']

When winter comes, Pete is in and out of the hospital with pneumonia and Larry brings the other men up to the hospital to visit him. Then there is that time Pete is in jail for public intoxication—the night he stood in the middle of Poplar Avenue and stopped traffic and then punched both Larry and the policeman who tried to move him out of the street. Pete sat in jail a few days for that one.

['For I was hungry, and you gave me meat: I was thirsty, and you gave me drink: I was a stranger, and you took me in: Naked, and you clothed me: I was sick, and you visited me: I was in prison, and you came unto Me.']

Another winter comes and Pete and his son, who had come up from Tupelo, Mississippi, got cold, really cold. They were sleeping on the porch of an out-of-business Mexican restaurant, and even though it doesn't get all that cold in Memphis too often, when it does, we Memphians have little tolerance for it—like five of the ten virgins in the Gospel, we are quite unprepared—and most of us tend to shiver all winter long and all of us complain with great vigor. People from the church give us sleeping bags and coats, but this particular cold spell requires more, with unwelcomed temperatures diving into the teens. It starts to snow, and the dilapidated porch of the Mexican restaurant does not provide enough shelter for this icy night. What Pete and his son need is a roof and some walls. I am asleep when Larry gets home.

Where have you been?

Those guys need more than a porch tonight, nobody should have to sleep in the snow. They are at the Comfortel on Summer Avenue. It's got heat and a warm shower. Now go back to sleep.

['I was homeless, and you gave Me a room.']

Insects and amphibians and crustaceans undergo the process of metamorphosis, which is a conspicuous and relatively abrupt change in the animal's body structure, accompanied usually by a change of habitat or behavior. Often, these creatures change into entirely different sorts of being. A caterpillar becomes a butterfly, and this process is nothing short of miraculous. After that night at the Comfortel, which ended up being three nights, a relatively long cold spell for Memphis, Pete begins a metamorphosis of his own.

Change is an odd thing, ironic in that we often cannot see change at the time it is actually occurring, we must observe the results of change after the fact. Such seeing often requires more of our attention than we can muster and a great deal of thoughtful inspection, otherwise, we can miss the change entirely. Pete's change looks like this: he starts giving Larry his government money.

The street folk of Memphis, at least the small handful we know, get a government check each month. Many of the street people also receive gifts from their families and, of course, there's the money they get from their work on the street. I don't know what they all do with this money—it's none of my business—but I know what Pete does; each month he either loses his money or people steal it from him or he spends it far too fast on liquor and cigarettes at the first of the month leaving himself nothing at all on the thirty-first. This was the formula of Pete's life, such as it was, month after month, year after year, until those snowy nights at the Comfortel. After those nights, I guess Pete figures that maybe he can trust this pastor-friend of his, and he starts giving Larry his money to manage. Larry takes Pete's government check each month and saves it for him in the bank. Then at the beginning of every week, Larry gives Pete one-quarter of the month's money. Try not to lose it, Pete, Larry says. Don't drink it all up, buddy. It's hard in the beginning, learning to trust someone to keep something important for you when virtually everyone you know has only taken from you. The learning curve is steep and trusting people again is a slow building project. But believe it or not, that's exactly what Pete begins to do, he begins to trust Larry to manage his money. Over some time, Pete loses his money less and less, and little by little he quits drinking it all up, little by little, he sobers up. Pete doesn't have a month's worth of cash in his pockets anymore, so other people on the street leave him alone—they don't steal from him as much because he doesn't have as much to steal.

Spring comes, as it always does, and the flowers bloom up red and white and yellow and purple and brand-new birds spring from their shells and Memphis warms back up. Pete finds his way back to the porch of the still-out-of-business Mexican restaurant, and Larry and Pete start riding around in the car again, picking up and delivering things for the church and having lunch at Burger King, the #1. Normal springtime stuff, like metamorphoses.

On one such warm afternoon, Larry approaches Pete with an offer that he certainly *can* refuse.

Pete, I've found you a place to stay, if you're interested. A home.

I got a place to stay, Pete mumbles, the porch at the restaurant suits me good.

Yes, I understand. But the place I've found could be permanent, if you want that. Warm in the winter and cool in the summer. You'd have your own bathroom and little kitchen. And the people of the church will help you get some furniture of your own. Would you like to see it? I can take you there today, if you like.

I don't know about that, Pete says, in almost a whisper. I'm used to the street.

Along the edges that separate Midtown and East Memphis stands an old dormitory-turned-into-housing for the underserved, the people of the street. Fifteen floors of hope and a second chance. The rooms are small, these old dorm rooms that once housed students at the University of Memphis now make room for people who could use a roof and four walls.

A home.

The Victorian philosopher Thomas Carlyle must have been thinking of Pete when he wrote the line, 'Such transitions are ever full of pain,' for the chasm between street-living and apartment-dwelling is enormous, and at times almost uncrossable. Like Moses and the Israelites standing on the banks of the Red Sea, some waters appear too deep and too wide to cross, especially when the enemy is ever at our back. But reluctantly, Pete agrees to give it a try. He moves into a freshly-painted apartment on the 5th floor with a bed and a table and microwave to warm stuff up and a little TV, all contributed by the people at the church.

Unlike the street, there are rules in this apartment complex, another hurdle and not a small one. No drinking and no smoking, no open containers (roaches and rats, you know), no drugs, a strict curfew. Get caught breaking any of the rules and *boom,* you're out for good, no questions asked. These are rough waters to cross and the stakes are high and all of this comes with a new financial arrangement. At the first of the month, Larry treks over to the apartment office and pays Pete's rent out of his monthly allowance—Pete is still getting used to this, it's hard—and then Pete gets a quarter of what's left over each Monday for the remainder of the month to spend as he will.

In the early days at the apartment complex, Pete occupies much of his time eyeballing his new neighbors with suspicion. He thinks the administration is stealing from him. He thinks everyone is cheating him, everyone out to get him. Dear Pete may never fully trust again, who knows.

afternoons

He still calls Larry most every day to complain about the rules at the apartment complex and the smells and the 'weird sketchy' people. He calls Larry most every day with questions about the money, and he constantly worries about people stealing from him—he probably always will. And he calls Larry to ask for a ride to the store or the post office or Burger King.

But now when he calls Larry, he's beginning to say *thank you.* Not every day, but some days.

For now, Pete stays put, stays off the street, stays sober, stays alive. He's crossed through the rough waters, and for the time being, he is home.

going to

funerals I

> Friendship...is not about survival but rather what gives value to our survival.
>
> C.S. Lewis

Miss Sally had two funerals and today is her second. The first funeral was a few weeks ago, just for her family. Larry and I stood with the few as Miss Sally's ashes were spread over the graves of her parents and then more were spread over the life-sized statue of the standard poodle she commissioned for her grave marker—Sally adored that dog. That day a cold wind blew from the north, so we were instructed by the funeral director to stand upwind, a thoughtful and correct idea although I was struck by the idea of how funny Miss Sally would have thought this was, all of us moving this-way-and-that so as to stay out of her way like we've always done with her, and I giggled out loud during the eulogy, snorted a little actually, but as I said, the wind was blowing so surely no one heard me.

I stood apart from the rest of the group. One of Sally's lady relatives asked me to take pictures of the ceremony and handed me her phone before she sat down. It is remarkable what one sees at a funeral—fear and joy and rage and wet eyes and dry ones and interest and the lack thereof and a healthy dose of humor mixed with agony extreme, all that human fallibility has to offer—a gorgeous mess we magnify and attempt to capture through the mechanics of a camera lens.

As if life could ever be tamed, even for one brief moment.

One woman on the second row wept loudly with no restraint, her veiny hands writhing in her lap, while the man beside her glanced at his watch with a stifled yawn while a skinny white dog trotted across the little bridge at the entrance of the cemetery while a tractor sat idle at the top of a fresh pile of dirt while a groundskeeper mowed the grass at the edge of the fence.

Life is brief and living and dying are unique and terrible and wonderful to each of us in our own peculiarity.

Today's funeral, Sally's second, is arranged by the neighbors for the neighbors. Today there are no ashes, just memories rising up from them, which can be among the most beautiful of things, but the wind blows again, indeed a gale as Miss Sally joins the other souls who have departed from Elmwood Cemetery—Shelby Foote and soldiers from the Civil War and civil rights leaders and a handful of Confederate Army generals and senators and, my favorites, the Martyrs of Memphis, Sisters Constance and Thecla and Hughetta and Frances,

OLEG CASSINI

She modeled for Oleg Cassini in NYC until her mother summoned her home saying, 'Southern girls don't do that sort of thing.'

who stayed and fought the yellow fever in the 1870s, an epidemic taking upwards of 200 souls a day, Sisters who cared for the orphaned and started a soup kitchen and kept my school open during the epidemic in Memphis.

Miss Sally joins an august group who have gone before her in the brilliant hope of life again.

There are only thirteen of us present today, so many of Miss Sally's neighbors already passed, as ours is an old neighborhood. Five or six metal walkers stand in the aisle of the small chapel at Elmwood. Larry and I are the youngest ones present by far, and we've already passed the half way mark. The weather is bad and alerts scream with regularity all morning on the phones of the old who refuse to turn their phones off or have forgotten how to, such weather that several of Sally's neighbors stayed home, afraid to drive in wind and rain.

Hazel brings pictures of Sally from her house, one a picture of Miss Sally at her debutante ball in 1947. Sally was a knockout, I mean really, like an old movie star with those deep red magnificent lips and heavy eyebrows. She modeled for Oleg Cassini for three weeks in NYC until, as the story goes, her mother summoned her home saying, 'Southern girls don't do that sort of thing.'

In the chapel, Jeanne plays 'Amazing Grace' on a piano so

old it lists a bit to the left like a sinking ship, an instrument long past any hope of retuning, but we thirteen sing with gusto anyway, a song everyone knows the words to. Our pitchy, out-of-tune voices fit the tinny piano notes to perfection and no one wants anything more than to be right here right now. I keep my eyes on Jeanne at the piano, enamored of her instrumentation—Jeanne plays with great aplomb like pianists did in churches years ago, with myriad flourishes and trills, lifting and lifting and lifting her hands from the keys like birds in flight and we sing accordingly, the best we can.

Larry reads Sally's favorite, Psalm 23, and we cry at the phrase 'my cup runneth over' because hers did and ours are and we all understand and feel the great power of collective love and the mystery of opening ourselves to the overflow. Miss Sally would love this, we all say, and please pass the tissues.

Betty tells a story about how Miss Sally welcomed her to the neighborhood with tea and cucumber sandwiches when she moved from Nashville. Those days are gone by the wayside, Betty cries. And Margaret, who worked at one time as a writer for the *Memphis Press Scimitar,* tells of Sally's visiting the elderly on Sunday afternoons with her large poodle and a tiny kitten in tow, patient animals for the old folks to pet. Margaret reports the old folks adored Sally, and we laugh at how Sally always called the elderly 'old folks' when she herself was older than most of the them and was the most offended when that adjective was directed her way. I tell the story about the romping wedding shower Miss Sally gave when my daughter was getting married and how Miss Sally was amenable to inviting the 'church people' but only the ones who knew how to drink because she was planning a real *pahty,* not some church social-potluck-sort-of-nonsense and I was to keep this in mind when creating the guest list.

Miss Sally had a *wicked* Southern accent, and we all try to mimic her in our storytelling but fail completely, as trying to impersonate Miss Sally is like attempting the voice of Flannery O'Connor or Eudora Welty or Miss Daisy. Miss Sally was in a category all her own, a true Southern dying breed—I mean no disrespect—above us in ways of elegance and charm and gentility, so we sit in the wonder of her.

Thirteen of us gathered to remember, through wind and rain.

I've been pondering the idea of friendship in the last years, what it really means to stick with someone through thick and thin, what it means to live a full and complete life in all of its times, good and bad. I conclude a real friendship is like a real marriage—for better or worse, in sickness and in health—those words mean something to me, and they meant something to Sally. C.S. Lewis writes that, like philosophy or art, friendship is unnecessary and that friendship is not about survival but rather what gives value to our survival. Sally's friendship added great value to my life, and I can only hope my life added to hers. I learned more about loyalty and personal strength from her than just about anyone I know. And that's how thirteen of us gather on a stormy day to love a woman who taught us about loving deeply, who taught us to love even through disappointment and pain because that's what life is about, real life anyway. Thirteen reasons why life is wonderful and friendship makes it better and true friends stick no matter what, especially through wind and rain.

My grandson Teddy likes me to tickle his face when he's falling asleep. He's a big boy now but he wants me to tickle his face anyway and I do because one day in the far-too-near future he will stop asking and I already know that day will sneak up on the both of us and without either of us realizing it, I will not be asked to tickle his face anymore. Ba, will you tickle my face? he whispers and I whisper Yes, of course I will and he whispers back, I knew you would.

Miss Sally was one of those about whom people said, I knew you would. Surely goodness and mercy followed her all the days of her life and she now dwells in the house of the Lord forever.

Amen.

speaking at

funerals II

And even to your old age I am he,
and even to white hairs will I carry you.
Isaiah 46:4

The January wind tears an icy path across the flatland of the bluff city where I live, determined, it seems, to rip the blooms right off the flower-bundles I wrestle from the back seat of my car to haul into the church. Protecting myself from the cold bite, I turn against the wind, lower my shoulders, and slug back to the car to lug out heavy armfuls of old wooden-framed photographs and the thin black purse my mother left on the passenger seat.

In a crisp manila folder on the passenger's seat lay my father's eulogy, printed on clean white sheets.

I slide onto the driver's seat and lean my head back for a quiet minute to catch a quick breath before the service begins, but the cruel winter wind blows the pleasant memories of my childhood into the car to vex me—my father's easy grin the night I won the talent show for piano, his early morning Bible reading, our corny sayings no one thought were funny but us—fine memories far too tender for me on the day

I am to deliver his eulogy.

Memories must tear us apart before they can heal us, I reason, but a gust of cold wind blows the exquisite pain of our more recent past into the car as well—my father's last labored breaths, hospice nurses checking his bluing feet, his parched mouth. These newer more torturous memories whip in to blend with the fine old ones, and together joy and suffering join inextricably as one cold breath and blow the pages of my father's eulogy onto the floorboard in careless disregard. I slam the car door against the onslaught, but some memories refuse to be shut out; mine whirl above me, alive in the cold, bitter air.

The poet Gerard Manley Hopkins penned the line, *I wake and feel the fell of dark, not day.*

Now I understand it.

I've wrestled with the writing of my father's eulogy, my last few days spent in an ancient, desperate struggle between control and passionate abandon, my trashcan brimming with frustrated half drafts. I feel my words need to be sophisticated and graceful and dignified like my father. The desire to honor this gentle man with the same nobility with which he lived consumes me. In the end, I choose elegance as the tone for my father's eulogy, and I set passion aside, but I know immediately I've made the wrong choice.

We all have our jobs. My preacher-brother will man the receiving line, his specialty, and thank the people for coming, and make a lovely speech of his own, and my mother's only job for this day will be simply to survive it. So, who then will arrange for food for the after-meal? (This is the South, funeral food is a real thing.) Who will keep the group on schedule, make sure everybody is in the proper place and on time to boot? Who will communicate with the funeral director about my father's makeup, smudged dramatically across his forehead during his transport to the church?

I am a Southern woman, a Tennessee daughter, and for the likes of me on funeral day there is much to attend to. *Important moments demand decorum,* I conclude; thus, tending to what I perceive as the proper role of the first-born on her father's funeral day, I will keep my emotions decent and in order so that others might lose theirs. This my duty and my calling.

As far as my eulogy is concerned, the recalling of stories about my father before an audience (the way he rubbed his thumb on the back my little hand, how he called me his *darling* daughter) seem too vulnerable for both the current state of my grief and my felt duties of the day. So, I write a careful, well-crafted eulogy instead. I avoid personal story and in the place of intimacy, I choose good words from *other's* pens—Tennyson and Steinbeck and C.S. Lewis and

King David, my kin in a long career as a reader and an English teacher. In my grief I trust these folks more than I trust myself to eulogize the finest of men who, for me, is beyond description.

Yet, in compiling the grander words of other writers, I neglect too many of my own. The borrowed sentiments on the final draft stand on their own sound merit, make no mistake—*Tis better to have loved and lost / Than never to have loved at all*—so I set aside the fact that I'd made a lesser choice and plod on.

The air in the car is cold. I glance at my inky pages littering the floorboard, blown all akimbo by winter's angry gusts, and take a long look in the rearview mirror and observe an older face looking back, a face who understands that, in just a few minutes, she will make the same choice again, for there remains no time to alter the words written on those sheets, and the reflection in the mirror that morning is in no emotional state to wing it.

By choosing to play it safe, that starched face in the mirror will miss a vulnerable moment of intimacy. She will miss abandon.

Well anyway, I reason with the mirror, who can expect me to tell a socially distanced, COVID-mitigated, masked-up group of mourners about the time my father, in the excruciating throes of dementia, raised a bottle of olive oil in one trembling hand and vegetable grater in the other and threatened the life of his caregiver? How I FaceTimed with him as my husband sped me to their house, my constant shouting 'I'm coming, I'll be right there!' through the phone, and how it took almost an hour to rid my father's shaky hands of their weaponry. How, when he finally calmed down a bit, my usually-gentle father looked into my eyes as his tears fell and asked, 'Wouldn't it be better if I just went on and died?' Wild with abandon and unrestraint that painful night, my father seemed ready to take the next steps on his journey.

But I—the one who knows that underneath my mother's grieving clothes she wears the thin, blue-silk necktie my father wore on their wedding day, the lovely remembrance she's kept with her all these years—I choose to protect myself and my emotions on my father's funeral day.

There's simply too much beauty here! so much love!

This is how I come to wrap myself in the careful words of other storytellers. I choose sophistication over abandon and control over vulnerability, and in so doing I join the throng of weary travelers before me who also succumbed to the siren song of self-protection.

This is the story I should have told at my father's funeral.

Before my parents' move to a retirement village, my family

spent weeks sorting through the accumulation of their sixty-two-year marriage. We packed up their life. On most of those long afternoons my father—affectionately called Geezer by us and everyone we know—mostly snoozed, quiet in his worn leather recliner, waking only to ask again and then again, What are we doing? and Where are we going? and Am I going too? But on one of those busy days in early spring, my father shuffled behind his squeaky metal walker to where I stood among the packing boxes. Can I help? By this time in his long journey with Parkinson's, Geezer had forgotten our names, but not us. Of course, you can help. I handed him a pair of dull scissors. He smiled and began to cut tiny pieces of duct tape from the roll and place the thin strips in neat little rows along the edge of the table, his engineer's mind still geared toward tidiness and order. We worked together in the pleasant quiet until I noticed his tears. Geezer, I whispered, taking his shaking hands, why are you crying? Do you know why you are so sad?

For the past months it had become clear that Geezer was taking care of his emotional affairs with what little locution he had left, speaking his last feeble phrases as his words betrayed him like his muscles had. He grasped my little hand in his large, wrinkled one and rubbed the back of my hand with his thumb. His weak lips labored to speak. Searching around in the darkening well of fading vocabulary, he looked at my little hand and found a few words to articulate his apprehension. Did this get worse? he asked.

Geezer had forgotten much, but he had *not* forgotten about my short little left arm with only three fingers. There was less support for mental and physical differences in those days; the language was harsher, with words like *birth defect* and *deformed* and *weird*. A young child once told me my hand looked like a Tyrannosaurus Rex's claw, and that kid was not too far off base. No one can deny the cruelty of children on the play yard and the meanness in the girls' locker room as children learn about showing kindness to others, or not, for we acknowledge that some folk never develop empathy, and in its stead choose violence and hatred to fill the void left by the absence of compassion.

And for all this, Geezer worried.

But things work out. I grew up a happy kid who married and bore a healthy child with ten fingers who in turn married and bore her own healthy child with ten. The mystic Julian of Norwich was correct in her reminder that 'all will be well and all manner of things will be well.' When we suffer, we participate with Christ in addressing the suffering in the world, and I realized only in the late stages of my father's life that he had borne my childhood suffering for me, vicariously. And now, before he forgot everything, Geezer sought the assurance that there was nothing more for him to do, to tell me he loved me by rubbing my little hand in farewell. To say goodbye.

Did this get worse? he asked again, his face faded in pain.

No, Geezer, it did not get worse, I whispered. It stayed the same. I grew up fine, I'm just fine.

He nodded. I knew you would be. His face relaxed into that old grin I loved so. I just knew it, he whispered.

Joy and suffering, in their extremes, are twin arms of the same steady compass, connected at the edges of love and abandon.

Geezer sat back down in his chair and closed his eyes.

present at the

eclipse

August 21, 2017 — Nashville

Nashville is an easy three-hour drive from Memphis straight up I-40 heading east, no need to stop for gas, and the Airbnb—a minimalist two-bedroom and bath situation in the upstairs of Superhost Jake's fine home—is equally easy to find in a neighborhood not far from a burger restaurant called Burger Up that Jake recommends as the best burger in Nashville and, since we've eaten so few burgers in Nashville before this (as, of course, fast food does *not* count), we take Jake up on his recommendation early that Sunday evening and discover that he is not wrong.

We've come to Nashville for the eclipse, my daughter Rainey and I tell every single person we meet: Jake at his house, our server at Burger Up, the people at the tables adjacent to us at Burger Up, the fellow beside us at the gas station, the fellow at the cash register at the gas station. We turn in for the evening in the comfy beds upstairs at Jake's house with the lone regret of not having any more people to tell why we've come to Nashville. But there's always tomorrow.

The eclipse begins at 10:58 am, ample morning time for sleep and a breakfast of croissants and blueberry jam and strong coffee with cream in Jake's kitchen before heading out to find our viewing spot, which turns out to be a large green space adjacent to a public library just west of downtown. I read that during the moments of totality, a 360° 'sunset' appears on the horizon as watchers stand in the enormous shadow of the moon, and this huge, flat lawn outside the library boasts few trees to obstruct our view. We are the first to arrive at this space, the first to park our car, and the first to plant two lawn chairs in the path of totality.

A small market stands not too far from the library lawn, so I leave Rainey to stake claim to our tiny patch of land as I saunter over to the store to buy some snacks and plenty of water.

Good morning, I say to the cashier, the only other person in the market.

Mornin', she replies back without looking up from her phone, can I help you?

Ahh, yet another person to tell why I am here in Nashville, my reason for being. Yes, I say, my daughter and I are in Nashville for the eclipse, and I've come to pick up water and some snacks. You are lucky, I continue with growing excitement, the eclipse is in your town *and* your store is located directly in the path of totality, isn't that amazing?!

afternoons

We've come from Memphis for the event, but all you have to do is walk right outside your door. Isn't that amazing?!

Only then does the lady look up from her phone. Is that today? she asks.

Incredulous, I yelp, Yes! and throw up my hands and keep going. The eclipse is today, right outside your door. The moment of totality is at 1:27, will you still be working at 1:27? Because if you are, all you have to do is step outside and look up and you will see it, amazing! Just step outside your door. By now I am almost shouting as another lady enters the store and stands at the head of the potato chip aisle to listen. Please tell me you'll go outside and take a look, I beg the clerk and the new lady now holding a bag of Cheetos.

We'll see, she says as she rings up my bill. Maybe I will, if I remember.

Maybe I will too, says the lady with the bag of chips.

Amazing.

By the time I arrive back to the library lawn it is 10:56, and an older man has joined us. He has a lawn chair but nothing else. My daughter and granddaughter are coming, the man explains, but I'm not sure when they will arrive. The eclipse begins in two minutes. Rainey and I have viewing-glasses and a pair of binoculars equipped to look at the sun. We put on our dark glasses and look up. The beginning of an eclipse is spectacular enough; a tiny sliver of the sun disappears and continues to disappear as the moon moves between the earth and sun, but nothing else changes. If you were not looking for it, you would not notice a difference. The older man has no viewing-glasses. His daughter and granddaughter have not yet arrived with his gear, or his lunch. We offer him cookies, which he accepts; we offer him binoculars, which he also accepts and looks up.

It is a cloudy day in Memphis, at my school, where girls gather on the soccer field after lunch to watch the eclipse. Memphis is not in the path of totality, only 97% rather than 100% for Memphis eclipse-watchers. St. Mary's girls play soccer and walk the track and sit on blankets to watch and wait, I'm told, hoping for the clouds to disperse.

But in Nashville, there are fewer clouds, and several hundred people begin to gather on the library lawn as the moon moves, as our galaxy moves around itself. People eat their lunches and the entire group listens to music, Johnny Cash's song 'Ring of Fire' is popular this afternoon. We speak to one another and loan binoculars and glance down at our books and up at the sky and check our phones for the timing and share our water and listen to the constant traffic *woosh* by on I-40 so close to the library, and we live together for a couple of hours on this lovely green lawn as if cosmic miracles happen every day. The older man's daughter and grand-daughter still have not arrived, so he joins us for hummus and carrot sticks and more chocolate chip cookies. What a lovely picnic! he says. I smile and eat a cookie and look up.

Already half of the sun is gone.

The mathematical accuracy and speed and predictability of celestial phenomena shakes me to the bone. Jupiter, the largest planet in our solar system, is quite far from Earth, 485.48 million miles to be exact, and ironically this enormous planet spins faster than any of the other planets, making one rotation around its axis in slightly under ten hours compared to Earth's twenty-four, spinning twenty-seven times faster than Earth at a whopping 28,324 miles an hour. Jupiter is so far away from the sun that it takes twelve Earth years for this giant ball to make its trip around the hot star of our solar system, and scientists know all these facts because they can see and measure these phenomena through the telescopes and probes and cameras that they themselves dreamed of and then drew and then engineered and then built.

It's no wonder ancient men erected the Tower of Babel; it seems we've always believed that with enough human ingenuity, we could actually reach God with human hands.

The dwarf planet Pluto takes 248 Earth years to orbit the sun and is 3.3152 *billion* miles from Earth—how can one begin to fathom such a distance!—and yet we have actual pictures of the surface of this small planet so far away from us because insanely brilliant NASA scientists understand the physics and the mathematics needed to build and send a spacecraft called New Horizons to explore distant Pluto up close. And if this isn't enough, in a matter of seconds I can find an actual photograph of Pluto's giant ice volcanoes on a device in my back pocket that children as young as my grandson carry around in *their* pockets all the livelong day.

But planetary movement aside, it is the eclipse that does me in. My phone tells me not only where and when to stand to best see totality—36.1627° N, 86.7816° W—which turns out to be a lovely park just outside of downtown Nashville at 1:27 pm on the dot. The precise mathematics of the universe convinces me anew that there is nothing random here. I find a map online which plots out the eclipse schedule for the years 2001-3000 in the United States, mathematically accurate for the next 1000 years and most certainly beyond. I remember a friend of mine in Belgium who looked up at the heavens and declared she saw only chaos; but considering the facts, I suppose I must view the stray asteroid as the anomaly rather than the norm. The gorgeous mathematical symmetry of the universe is so far far away from my limited human understanding, but its song seems to be one of order and arrangement and beauty—the universe sings of a Creator.

I do not have to understand this symmetry in order to believe it.

At 1:25, only two short minutes before totality, the crowd quiets as color of the known world changes. The trees and grass, once green, have now turned into a tintype, a mere photograph on a thin sheet of metal. The old man's daughter has arrived just in time for the big moment, but her skin is gray, her teeth silver like an old woman almost dead, how fearsome this mother must appear to her young daughter who cannot see that her own skin has also turned gray as a corpse. I look away from this bleak, colorless land and up to the darkening heavens where the sun is now gone, replaced by a diamond ring, a thin circle of fire holding an enormous bright gem, still too brilliant to look at with human eyes.

The old man's granddaughter moans and begins to cry. Her colorless mother picks her up and whispers *it's OK, baby*, but it isn't; the birds have fled and in their stead the evening crickets chirp in the growing deep blue-black sky and the children feel it and quieten, or wail. The day is night and the world is upside down and all color has fled. I turn to the horizon for light and in great relief I see the glow, a 360° sunset encircling us entirely as the moon covers the sun, running orange and red along the flat surface of the earth, and yet this is no country for comfort, for in an instant the black shadow of the moon roars at us from all sides like a heavy black drape, covering the daylight with thick darkness from which we cannot escape. A baby screams and her mother weeps.

Shadows appear on the ground in skinny wavy black crescent-shaped parallel lines. Since the sun is so dramatically reduced as a light source during a total eclipse, the little light available casts shadows of the Earth's atmospheric winds onto the floor of the Earth, crescent-shaped wind patterns gather at my feet as if it's an ordinary day.

The temperature drops six degrees. Johnny Cash still sings low but no one is listening, for we are holding our breath and listening for the trumpet call announcing the end of days. Bright stars come out in sudden great battalions and lovely Venus appears next to the giant hole in the sky and beside me a woman gasps and covers her mouth in terror, or joy—it's impossible to know the difference. I look up and the sun is no more. I take off my glasses and see nothing but a flat black disc in the sky, a black hole that swallowed the sun, and both heaven and earth are cold, and silent.

This is the way the world ends.

After ninety-six seconds, the moon moves and sun returns and lights the darkness as she did on Creation's fourth day.

The crowd quiets as the black shadow of the moon covers the daylight with thick darkness from which we cannot escape.

Let there be light, again. Perhaps ninety-six seconds is all we can stand of glory, or miracle, or awe, for now I know the line between joy and terror is thin indeed. Eyes toward the heights, we watch the black hole shrink into a crescent of its own and the earth warms, again. The babies quiet and the birds return. It is finished, and I am sad.

The crowd disperses far faster than it gathered. Our clocks read 1:28 now—oh, how one's world can change in two minutes, nay, not even two!—and all these busy people have places to go, places to be. We gather our belongings. I turn to say good-bye to the old man but he and his family have disappeared. By the time we get to our car, things move back toward normal. How quickly we move from the miraculous to glance down at our phones, a very poor trade as we all know. I pull onto I-40 West toward Memphis, as I must, and my daughter hangs out of the car window for a long while, glasses on and face skyward, watching the other side of the eclipse.

I hope the lady at the market walked outside, just for a minute.

The longest total solar eclipse to occur between the dates of 4000 BC and at least 6000 AD (10,000 years) will be on July 16, 2186, a Sunday, with a duration of 7 minutes and 29.22 seconds of totality. The longest historical solar eclipse lasted 7 minutes, 27.54 seconds on June 15, 743 BC.

The longest eclipse possible for the third millennium is 7 minutes and 32 seconds. I'll not be around here for any of these, but perhaps I will witness these miracles from another vantage point.

We are fortunate. The next eclipse for us is just around the bend, April 8, 2024, and while the city of Memphis once again does not lie in the path of totality, we are not far off the path. In this eclipse, the longest duration of totality will be 4 minutes and 26 seconds in Arkansas and central Texas at 1:30 local time. I'll be there, although I'm not sure my fragile heart or my weak knees can survive more than 96 seconds of glory.

We will have to see. I'll bring a defibrillator and knee pads.

I can hardly wait. I'll see you there.

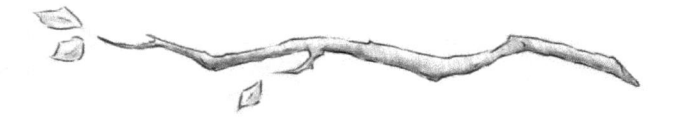

remember to

dance

> Those who were seen dancing were thought to be
> insane by those who could not hear the music.
> Frederich Nietzsche

WILLIE In the hot Memphis summertime, on our back porch, we listen to Willie Nelson—not exclusively Willie, mind you, but there are significant stretches of time when our evening music is nothing but. That easy, crooning voice of his, there's just something about his toney baritone I can't get enough of. Especially in the summertime, especially on my back porch where the water streaming through our little copper fountain blends with that slow sliding twang of Willie's voice and the early evening sky glows pink-and-orange and I believe all over again that tiny moments of beauty exist around us all the time, moments of glory where the music meets the water meets the sunset meets the lover's hand meets the warm summer air meets the child's still-small voice meets the memory of my beloved father meets the promise found in the mellow voice of a mere man singing words I believe and hope he does as well:

Some day when we meet up yonder
We'll stroll hand in hand again
In a land that knows no parting
Blue eyes crying in the rain.

TEDDY But our back porch is not built for country music only, she enjoys other music as well—show tunes come to mind—and one evening in the early fall my grandson is sitting with me on the porch when the song 'I Could Have Danced All Night' shuffles its way into my show tunes playlist, and I remember the days so many years ago when I directed the musical *My Fair Lady* and sweet Amy Redden sang Eliza Doolittle's song so beautifully, and I smile all over again at the glory of good memories and start to sing the words out loud and my grandson asks me if I know this song and I say yes and then he asks the question I hope he will ask me again and again and again:

Ba, will you dance with me?

Yes, I will, little boy.

We jump up from the couch and clasp hands, and while we twirl and skip and hop and fling our arms all about the back porch like two whirling dervishes in the divine frenzy of dance and love for each other and the glory of the moment, yes, this very moment! and I sing these words to the top of my voice:

I'll never know what made it so exciting
Why all at once my heart took flight,
I only know when he began to dance with me
I could have danced, danced, danced all night.

For what else am I to do?

The glory of the moment is in the moment itself, never in the moment to come.

PEONY In my exercise class is an elderly lady who, as the story goes, was a professional ballerina in her younger years. She comes to the Saturday morning class when she comes, but sadly, she is no longer a regular. I haven't seen her now for months and months. Her name is the name of a flower—not Rose or Iris or Violet but something more like Pansy or Daisy or Peony—yes, Peony, I think. Rather than practicing all the crunches and tucks and sit-ups and push-ups in a normal class, Peony stays at the barre for most of the session, just dancing. She participates in her way, lifting her arms and legs as she will, when she will. Peony rarely makes it down to the floor for the abs workout, but rather she undulates around her own space in the corner of the room, her arms lift and lower and lift again at the barre like gentle waves caressing the shoreline of the sea, or like a glorious thin willow branch swaying in the wind at the frail edges of memory. But make no mistake, Peony's still got what it takes.

I'm not absolutely positive on this point, but it seems as if Peony is particularly energetic when the instructors choose 'girl-power' songs to play in class. Peony dials it up a notch every time Alicia Keys arrives on the scene, 'This girl is on fire!' and she feels it all over again when The Pussycat Dolls ask, 'Don't cha wish your girlfriend was hot like me? Don't cha?'

I spoke with Peony only once, the day she walked out of class with me into the warm sun, the day she talked for a long time about her love for dance and the ballet studio she helped to start and how she plans to dance every day until the day she dies; 'I've always danced, always will,' she declared to me that sunny day, 'and why would I not?' Now *there's* a proper question for you; why would anyone choose not to dance?

I haven't had the heart to ask if anyone at the exercise studio knows what has happened to Peony—I couldn't bear to hear any bad news about her. But if I ever do see Peony again, I will invite her over to dance with us on our back porch. The music's good and I feel sure she will fit right in.

GLORY   The poet declares:

> *The world is charged with the grandeur of God.*
> *It will flame out, like shining from shook foil…*
> *Because the Holy Ghost over the bent*
> *World broods with warm breast and ah! bright wings.*

God's glory, His grandeur is here for the seeing, for those with eyes to see.

POETRY Teddy wrote and recited his first poem to our small den filled with grandparents, his poem entitled 'Run':

Watch me run
When I run, I go very fast
The wind rushing past me
My feet going back and forth
I love to run.

This kid understands the glory of a moment, his young boy-face glowing with the stuff of sheer joy as he looks around the room at his elders cheering and clapping and grinning in delight at the boy who already knows that this bent old world is *charged* with the grandeur of God, so why not let your body love what it loves. If you love to run, for Heaven's sake, run boy run!

MUSIC The first concert Larry and I ever went to together was Willie Nelson at the Mid-South Coliseum in the late 1970s, a concert where Willie brought his pals Waylon Jennings and Crystal Gayle along just for fun. Before Willie, I had only been to two other concerts in my life—the first was The Monkees concert with my aunt Vicky and a clutch of her high school girlfriends who drove up from Central Mississippi and screamed and cried and danced all through the concert and waved their arms and declared their undying love to lead singer Davy Jones, swearing together through rivers of hormonal teenage tears that they would never marry anyone if they couldn't marry Davy Jones. And I believed them, for how could one disbelieve such devotion?

And the second concert was Bobby Sherman with my friend Kay Manley (who's now a super cool DJ on our favorite country music station KIX 106) and her sister Joy at the auditorium in downtown Memphis. Their parents dropped us off and we found our seats and Bobby Sherman came out in a purple-fringe suit (again, it was the early 70's) and sang 'Julie, Do Ya Love Me' and all I could imagine was that he was singing to me and I, in love, sang loud along with him and danced and substituted my name with Julie's. Yes, I love you, Bobby, with all my heart. Kay's mom and dad remember that we girls had on so much perfume they could hardly breathe in the car ride downtown, but it was Bobby Sherman, so what else were we to do?

The Willie and Waylon concert was another thing entirely, as one might imagine. Before that concert I'd never smelled the skunky smell of marijuana and I wondered aloud to Larry why the air was 'so smoky' and the gray-ponytailed middle-aged man sitting in front of us laughed hard and loud and held up a stumpy cigarette and asked me if I wanted a 'toke,' which I politely declined. Yet it was neither the offer of a toke nor the concert venue itself nor the thrill of the first days of dating a new guy that I remember the most from that evening—it was Willie, himself, and the joy on his face as he played, his slanty seductive grin when he harmonized with Waylon, and the clear delight he so obviously felt in simply strumming his guitar and cruising around the stage to his own music and doing what he loves with his whole heart. Oh, and of course the older couple who stood in the aisle nearest us, slow-dancing, swaying to the music.

What if every time we feel like fighting, we try dancing instead?

Not long ago I found a video of Willie playing and singing with his sons, his two boys, and I watched it far too many times on my back porch with tears streaming. At one point Willie's son sings 'Blue Eyes Cryin' in the Rain' and Willie, in what seems to be a surprise to his son, closes his eyes and starts to harmonize and the look of delight on that son's face when his father's voice blends in perfection with his own is impossible to translate into words, nothing short of sheer, raw, perfect delight.

POETRY   The poet Jack Gilbert declares, 'We must risk delight. We can do without pleasure, but not delight,' a thought to which I can offer nothing more than a heartfelt *Amen*.

MUSIC   Recently we attended a concert *far* outside the norm of our ordinary musical choices. The band Shinedown was

afternoons

in concert in Memphis at the FedEx Forum and one of the band members, Zach Myers, attends our church and generously gave us passes for the concert. To say this concert was extravagant understates the scene entirely; pyrotechnics (lots of fire!) and screaming guitars and a grand piano lowered down onto the stage and then raised back up to the rafters and our friend playing and singing his heart out and 18,000 screaming fans and four fabulous musicians on stage risking delight, loving what they love and doing it with all their heart. But they weren't the only ones—the crowd, ah, the crowd. We stood on a raised platform facing the stage so I could turn around and around and watch the crowd and hear them sing and watch them dance and listen as they cheered for their hometown hero, a Memphis boy named Zach whom they adore, a musician who was surprised with a key to his city that night, and the crowd erupted in shouts and jumps and song as they joined the gleeful joy-dance for this man they love and the music he creates.

But not only that. As I watched Zach play and sing, I realized that the very next night another 18,000 fans, an entirely different group of people, would gather again in this same venue with the same electricity, cheering this time for our hometown team the Memphis Grizzlies as they play the Lakers in the NBA playoffs—Memphis has its faults, but city-pride is not one of them—and once again the very beams of this massive steel forum will dance and buzz with the energy of excited people simply loving what they love.

WILLIE

Some day when we meet up yonder
We'll stroll hand in hand again
In a land that knows no parting
Blues eyes crying in the rain.'

Willie's words have staying power, these words remain to be sung again and again because this is the cry of our collective heart—not only the 'blue eyes crying' part, which we understand all too well, but the 'someday meeting up yonder in a land that knows no parting' part, for the glory of this hope not only redeems loss but shimmers in the fullness of the glory to come, glory so rich and so unfathomable and so palpable that we can stand only tiny threads of it while we still live and breathe down here in these parts.

MUSIC OF THE NIGHT Last night I woke to the percussive hooting of night creatures, two huge owls in a pre-dawn conversation right outside my bedroom window. The moon is bright, its milky glow flows through the slats in my bedroom shutters across the wood floor in streamers of night-light, and I stumble in the dark to take a look outside. Just beyond the window panes, atop the steep slant of my neighbor's roof, I see the black silhouette of an enormous owl backlit by the white spotlight of a full springtime moon.

afternoons

This bird is lifting his legs and turning his heavy body in circles, dancing in the moonlight. Somewhere out of sight—I think atop *my* roof—is another owl hooting her love song in return. For a full fifteen minutes, these two sing the night away, hoot the morning flowers into bloom, dance the stars to their beds, and awaken the warm sun from her eastern resting place to travel once again across the grand blue canvas of the sky.

I hear a noise and glance away for a tiny second and when I look back through the shutter slats, the owl is gone. A simple blink and I miss his leaving. I sting with regret that I did not see his vast and mighty wings lift his own heavy body into the bluing—I must better learn how to stay awake.

Soon the sparrows will begin their morning song, but for a few quiet moments in the thick silence between darkness and light, we human fledglings rise from our restful nests into the dawn of a brand-new day to sing Nature's great resurrection song, or to refuse to. The song whose lyrics promise the good news that day follows night, peaks follow valleys, and glory follows anguish.

DREAM In my dream last night, I am standing on a gigantic wooden lifeboat sailing eastward toward an unknown land. The west wind blows hearty and pushes the lifeboat onward, over and through the heights and depths of great sea swells, but I find I have no fear. Willie Nelson stands at the bow of the boat strumming and singing

Blue skies smiling at me
Nothing but blue skies, do I see

and Bobby Sherman stands at the stern harmonizing with Willie and these two fine musicians grin at each other and wink as they play, relishing with great joy the music in their fingers and on their lips, and Kay Manley and I and her sister Joy slow-dance in the middle of the boat beside Peony who is dancing *en pointe* alongside us, twirling her toile skirts in the early evening breezes as the sun wanes. Beside Willie in the front of the lifeboat, my grandson stands and recites his newest poem entitled 'Still Running,' and Shinedown and the Memphis Grizzlies gather together along the gunwales of the vessel with their legs hanging over the edges and they all begin to splash their feet (and each other!) in the warm seawater. All souls on board splash and sing and dance to the music and applaud the poetry and the slow moon rises to give his blessing to it all.

As we near the far shore, those two big owls from my yard fly in, their dark and mighty wings flapping in synchrony, and these birds greet us with their heavy hoots of low-decibeled song and make a breezy landing on the gunwales right beside where Shinedown and the Grizzlies sit splashing their feet.

At the setting of the sun, just before dark night replaces bright day, Willie tunes his guitar for Vespers. We travelers on this lifeboat collectively lift our heads toward the unknown shore and Willie sings us in:

> *Blue days, all of them gone*
> *Nothing but blue skies from now on.*

Look up, your redemption draweth nigh!

GLORY We human beings yearn for the gifts of God; we are created for them. Like a baby at the breast, we long for delight, like explorers in a New World, we continue to search for joy while standing among all our broken temporal things, and ironically, we feel the weight of glory most profoundly when we sorrow most.

These moments in our normal lives when suddenly the veil is pulled back for the merest blink of an eye and we know, in those fleeting, fragile moments when we can see feel touch taste hear the glory that surrounds us, we know there is more. Glory, the weight of which is so magnificent it would crush us if we had any more than the thinnest glimpse of it, Glory that redeems brokenness, Glory that is but a shimmer, a glimmer of the Promised Land beyond our own, a Land so bright it must be veiled lest we as mere mortals actually see its fullness with human eyes, and die.

But I am convinced, more than ever, that the veil is thinning.

epilogue

Early in the summer of his seventh year, the little boy proclaims he wants to plant a garden in his yard and watch it grow. And not just a garden in pots, he declares with all the moxie and forthrightness of a first-time farmer; no pots like the ones we use for mere herbs or flowers (as if a flower or herb could ever be considered 'mere'!) for this boy, no sir. He wants to plant a real garden in the *ground*, in the hard earth that he digs up himself with a shovel and tills with a rake and fertilizes and waters with his own two hands and watches grow with his own two eyes.

So, the boy's grandparents, Larry and I (Lad and Ba) take the little boy to Lowe's and purchase potting soil and fertilizer and bug spray and stones to line the edges of the garden and two handfuls of envelopes containing a variety of seeds. Then we cart all our gear and tackle and hopes and dreams to the tiny 5 x 5 plot of dirt between the little boy's house and our own, and the boy and his grandfather start digging.

And a farmer is born.

Digging is hard work, the little boy says as he chops at the earth with a spade. It is, Lad replies as he pushes his grandfather Joe's old shovel hard into the crunch of the dry dirt. But most of the time the things that require the hardest work yield the best reward, Lad says. Those two fellows read the instructions on the back of the seed packets and follow them precisely, and although the little boy grows overly excited a time or two and pours too many seeds into many of the two-inch-deep holes they poke into the soil with their fingers, nonetheless the man and the boy plant tomatoes and beans and carrots and cucumbers and radish seeds all afternoon and then they drag out the hose and water the rich black dirt into mud before they go inside exhausted, ready for a cool bath and a warm bed.

The morning after the planting, from my window I spot the young Boy–Farmer standing by his garden in the early morning pink light just staring at the soil, so I join him with a cup of hot coffee in hand. Nothing has grown yet, Ba, he declares. No, I say, but it hasn't yet been one whole day. The best things take time, good things take a while to grow, you know. Like you.

Yes, like me, he says.

For a week or two or three, the little boy checks his garden four or five times a day, his hands on his skinny knees looking looking looking for anything green, for even the tiniest hint of a sprout, but nothing comes. I'm not sure my vegetables are going to grow, Ba, the first-time-Boy–Farmer says, slightly glum, and I say, we must be patient. To produce the best of things takes a great deal of time.

epilogue

And then one morning, after a terrific pop-up rain storm that we all watched from our back porches, concerned that the rain would simply *whoosh* the boy's tender seeds right down the driveway and into the raging river running down the gutter toward the ditch, the little boy rushes out and checks his garden and there it is, a first sprout—the tiny bright green sprig of a radish leaf.

The boy jumps and whoops and spins around his small garden like a leprechaun who, after much diligent searching, finally finds the pot of gold at the end of the rainbow.

Since that time, the little boy's garden has exploded in growth. The cucumber vines—whose leaves are now the size of dinner plates and crawling onto the driveway and into the branches of the neighboring bushes—produce more yield than the boy's family can possibly eat, so the Boy–Farmer gives many of his cucumbers away to the neighbors just like his great-great-grandfather Joe did, neighbors who all smile and brag on the size of the cucumbers and encourage the young farmer in his work. *And how are your tomatoes doing, Teddy?* the neighbors ask. *They are growing great!* Much to the boy's delight, many afternoons we eat the cherry tomatoes right off the vine, and just yesterday the boy pulled up his first carrots, two rich orange miracles tugged gently from the dark ground below us, and we ate them immediately, dirt and all.

This is more than I *ever* thought would grow! the young Boy–Farmer shouts in the sheer, sublime glory of creation and the result of the hard work of his hands. I just planted little tiny seeds, but now the plants are *huge* and we actually made food, it's a miracle!

This Boy–Farmer understands the miracle of sowing and reaping, an idea many of us post-modern folk can forget (or reject or sometimes even scorn) as we collectively remove our hands from the miraculous soil and place our grip instead on temporal things that rust and break and disconnect us from each other and the earth. The ancient prophet Isaiah proclaims that 'a little child shall lead us,' and his prophecy resounds not only through the millennia but all the way to this small street in Memphis where a young Boy–Farmer reminds his parents and grandparents and all his neighbors each and every day of the law of the harvest—that what we put in is what we get out.

But more, always more.

Do you know that we always reap *more* than we sow? the Boy–Farmer's mother asks him one day while they water the garden. That is the system in place, she continues, Creation's way of being. You planted cucumber seeds so tiny you could barely see them, but now the cucumbers are larger than your father's hand, and the bright red tomatoes are so sweet and plentiful. We always reap more than we sow.

I just planted little tiny seeds, but now the plants are huge and we actually made food, it's a miracle!

It's true, the Boy–Farmer confirms.

And not everything grows at the same pace or with the same vigor, the Boy–Farmer's mother observes. The snap beans and the radishes and the carrots are producing much more slowly than the cucumbers and tomatoes, but does the rate of their growth lessen their beauty or importance? Just because one vegetable grows and changes faster than another, does that make that vegetable better?

No, it does not, the Boy–Farmer confirms again. Plus, I don't even like cucumbers.

His mama smiles and nods. So, what has your garden taught you, or shown you? she asks.

That everything grows at different times and in different ways, the Boy–Farmer offers, only a bit unsure in his response.

Yes, his mama says, that's it. So, we shouldn't judge the growth of the fruits of the garden, should we? Or even the birds at the feeder or the squirrels in the yard or our friends at school because everything grows and behaves and blooms in different ways and at different speeds, right?

That's right, says the little boy.

I grew up thinking or believing that the phrase 'you reap what you sow' was primarily a negative idea, and now I can't imagine why, because my parents didn't think or teach this

epilogue

way, but somehow in my early years, the phrase sounded to me more like a threat or some odd form of control. *You better watch out, for you reap what you sow.* I suppose it can be (or has been) preached that way, for much depends upon tone, does it not?

But alas, sowing and reaping is one of the elemental systems of this old world of ours, a good system that makes logical sense. If I sow cucumbers, guess what I'll get? Not tomatoes or carrots or peas or radishes. I will harvest cucumbers because I reap what I sow.

This system applies to the metaphysical as well. The prayer of Saint Francis comes to mind, he understood this idea quite well:

> *Lord, make me an instrument of your peace:*
> *Where there is hatred, let me sow love;*
> *Where there is injury, pardon;*
> *Where there is doubt, faith;*
> *Where there is despair, hope;*
> *Where there is darkness, light;*
> *Where there is sadness, joy.*

What a beautiful sentiment! we all say and place these words in our prayer books and on our refrigerators. But according to the rules of this system of reaping and sowing combined with the existential profundity of human choice, the law must accommodate itself in both directions—'where there is faith, let me sow doubt,' must then also be available, as well as 'where there is light, darkness,' or 'where there is pardon, injury'—but I have neither the energy nor the desire to write out the rest of *that* list. You will have to sort that one out for yourself.

It is simple, really. I will get back what I give.

Perhaps the best part of the miracle of sowing and reaping, though, is that it supersedes time, therefore it's never too late to start or to start over for the better. We can begin sowing well at any time and at any age. If I sow the fruit I want to receive, if I start now, this very day, then I *will* reap if I don't faint.

And sometimes, miraculously, we even reap what we did not sow—kindness instead of cruelty, forgiveness despite the hurt, generosity instead of greed. And therein lie the greatest miracles of all—mercy, grace, and love.

This particular little Boy–Farmer is dwelling and growing happily in the morning of his life—his one and only childhood—that blessed morning where the sun always shines even on rainy days and the lines are clear and he is safe and most days are happy ones and there is miracle.

epilogue

The little boy's parents live and thrive in the glory of their afternoon, that remarkable period of maturity and great growth and change and metamorphosis—a time of developing into even more of whom they were uniquely created to be and realizing, with joy immeasurable, how very beautiful it is to be alive and to realize anew that there is miracle.

And the little boy's grandparents, Lad and Ba, we who have reached the early evening of our time on this good earth, that glorious dusk where our hands are still able to work in the dirt and the sand, when we are still planting and replanting and inventing and doing and redoing and giving and forgiving like some people do when they realize there is less of life yet to live than has already been lived, and that fact doesn't worry us at all but rather excites us and gives us more reasons to wake up joyful and aware that each moment is a gift and a glory and there is always miracle.

When the farmer-poet Wendell Berry was asked why farmers still farm, given the difficult conditions and the economic adversity, he famously responded, 'Love. They must do it for love.' Oh, amen and amen. For how we spend our days, of course, is how we spend our lives.

So, let us spend our mornings evenings and afternoons sowing love, bountifully, so that we may reap the same, and every day proclaim the beauty of the earth and sky and the sun and moon and the glorious stars and delight in our fellow sojourners on this spinning globe.

So, love.

Sow love.

For at the end of the day, in thunder or in clear skies, each life is a miracle. And a Glory.

תִּפְאֶרֶת

acknowledgements

More than thanks to my friends and family who encourage me daily to write my stories down. It took me a while to get started, but now I'm here to stay.

Special thanks to my good friend Leigh Mansberg who reminded me, in my throes of despair over a patch of unsuccessful work on a novel, that some of the best writers of all were essayists and that I should be proud of my own strong voice. Good advice for us all and a kick in the pants for me.

To my friend Albert Throckmorton who volunteered, on a whim, his expert services as an editor and proofreader and found so many ways to make these stories stronger. You may have opened Pandora's box, Albert, for there's more a'coming.

To my friend Jenny Madden who, once on a trip to Ireland, asked me what I was waiting for.

To St. Mary's Episcopal School, my place, for so many years of love and care. And to Christ Community Church for the same.

To my brilliant publisher Rip Coleman who keeps giving me a chance.

To Sarah for art that continues to enhance these stories beyond my wildest thoughts.

To Nanny and Geezer who showed us all how to love.

And to Lad, for all these good years.

about the author

A teacher of literature and writing in the Memphis area for nearly forty years, Shari Brand Ray is currently English Department Chair at St. Mary's Episcopal School in Memphis. A native Memphian, Shari enjoys taking long walks on the Greenline, teaching English, and writing on her back porch while she watches the birds. Infusing verse throughout much of her prose, Ray leans on the shoulders of the great poets for both truth and inspiration. After a lifetime of writing down stories, her first book, *Surprised by Imperfection,* was released in 2022.